The Hopi

The Hopi

William W. Lace

LUCENT BOOKS
SAN DIEGO, CALIFORNIA

THOMSON
GALE

Detroit • New York • San Diego • San Francisco
Boston • New Haven, Conn. • Waterville, Maine
London • Munich

LIBRARY OF CONGRESS CATALOGING-IN-PUBLICATION DATA

Lace, William W.
   The Hopi / by William W. Lace.
        p. cm. — (Indigenous peoples of North America)
Summary: Discusses the history, daily lives, culture, religion, and conflicts of
the Hopi Indians.
Includes bibliographical references and index.
   ISBN 1-59018-086-0 (hardback : alk. paper)
   1. Hopi Indians—History—Juvenile literature. 2. Hopi
Indians—Social life and customs—Juvenile literature. [1. Hopi Indians.
2. Indians of North America—Arizona.] I. Title. II. Series.
   E99.H7 L23 2003
   979.1004'9745—dc21

                                                                2002001836

Contents

Foreword

North America's native peoples are often relegated to history—viewed primarily as remnants of another era—or cast in the stereotypical images long found in popular entertainment and even literature. Efforts to characterize Native Americans typically result in idealized portrayals of spiritualists communing with nature or bigoted descriptions of savages incapable of living in civilized society. Lost in these unfortunate images is the rich variety of customs, beliefs, and values that comprised—and still comprise—many of North America's native populations.

The *Indigenous Peoples of North America* series strives to present a complex, realistic picture of the many and varied Native American cultures. Each book in the series offers historical perspectives as well as a view of contemporary life of individual tribes and tribes that share a common region. The series examines traditional family life, spirituality, interaction with other native and non-native peoples, warfare, and the ways the environment shaped the lives and cultures of North America's indigenous populations. Each book ends with a discussion of life today for the Native Americans of a given region or tribe.

In any discussion of the Native American experience, there are bound to be sim-

ilarities. All tribes share a past filled with unceasing white expansion and resistance that led to more than four hundred years of conflict. One U.S. administration after another pursued this goal and fought Indians who attempted to defend their homelands and ways of life. Although no war was ever formally declared, the U.S. policy of conquest precluded any chance of white and Native American peoples living together peacefully. Between 1780 and 1890, Americans killed hundreds of thousands of Indians and wiped out whole tribes.

The Indians lost the fight for their land and ways of life, though not for lack of bravery, skill, or a sense of purpose. They simply could not contend with the overwhelming numbers of whites arriving from Europe or the superior weapons they brought with them. Lack of unity also contributed to the defeat of the Native Americans. For most, tribal identity was more important than racial identity. This loyalty left the Indians at a distinct disadvantage. Whites had a strong racial identity and they fought alongside each other even when there was disagreement because they shared a racial destiny.

Although all Native Americans share this tragic history they have many distinct differences. For example, some tribes and individuals sought to cooperate almost immediately with the U.S. government while others steadfastly resisted the white presence. Life before the arrival of white settlers also varied. The nomads of the Plains developed altogether different lifestyles and customs from the fishermen of the Northwest coast.

Contemporary life is no different in this regard. Many Native Americans—forced onto reservations by the American government—struggle with poverty, poor health, and inferior schooling. But others have regained a sense of pride in themselves and their heritage, enabling them to search out new routes to self-sufficiency and prosperity.

The *Indigenous Peoples of North America* series attempts to capture the differences as well as similarities that make up the experiences of North America's native populations—both past and present. Fully documented primary and secondary source quotations enliven the text. Sidebars highlight events, personalities, and traditions. Bibliographies provide readers with ideas for further research. In all, each book in this dynamic series provides students with a wealth of information as well as launching points for further research.

The Fight for Survival

Arizona's Indian Route 2 runs straight, flat, and lonely from the Navajo town of Leupp northward toward the villages of the Hopi. The land is almost barren, both of vegetation and people. The road skirts the Painted Desert on the east. Beyond the desert, near the city of Flagstaff, the San Francisco Mountains soar to a height of more than 12,500 feet.

About fifteen miles north of Leupp, the road leaves the Navajo reservation and enters the Hopi Nation. There is no sign—nothing to mark the boundary, one forced on the Hopi, and one they do not recognize as valid.

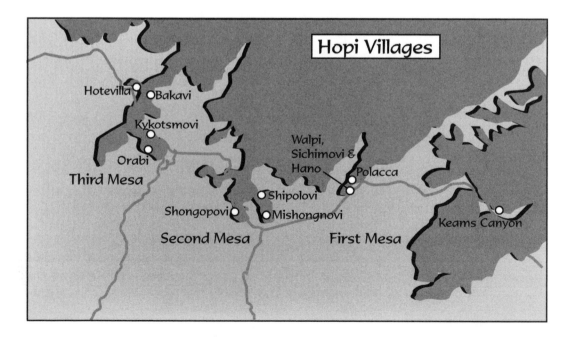

The road gradually rises, emptiness on either side, for another twenty miles before the heart of Hopi country comes into view. It first appears as a dark line on the horizon. This is the southern edge of Black Mesa, part of the huge Colorado Plateau that extends northward another two hundred miles into Utah.

The Three Mesas

Three rocky fingers extend south from Black Mesa—First Mesa on the east, Second Mesa in the middle, then Third Mesa—so named because this was the order in which the white man encountered them. Perched high atop the mesas or huddled at their bases are the eleven villages of the Hopi. Two more are miles to the west, off the Hopi Reservation and surrounded by the Navajo.

From below, it is sometimes difficult to make out the mesa-top villages, even if one knows they are there. Built for the most part of the same yellowish sandstone as the mesas, they seem to have grown out of the earth itself—creations of nature instead of humans.

Some villages are new, but many—those on the mesas, especially—are ancient. The oldest inhabited village, Orabi, dates from about A.D. 1150, making it the oldest continuously inhabited town in North America. Other, even older, villages lie in ruins here and there.

The older villages are built apartment-style, often multistory, the houses sharing common walls. Some, centuries old, were built with the rocks and boulders that abound at the foot of the mesas. Paved streets are rare. There is an ancient feel, so the occasional modern touch—a satellite dish atop a five-hundred-year-old house—is a shock.

The landscape changes as the three-hundred-foot climb to the mesa tops is made. Below, the soil is sandy, having been blown north to collect in dunes at the base of the mesas. Here, most of the farming takes place. Above, covered with short tough rabbit brush and dotted with juniper trees, the land is more suitable to grazing. While summers are mild at this elevation—about sixty-five hundred feet above sea level—winters can be harsh.

Water, or lack of it, is an eternal Hopi problem. Rainfall averages only about eleven inches a year. When the rains have not come, as has happened often in past centuries, the crops have failed and the people have starved. Little wonder that so much Hopi ritual centers around rainfall.

A Threatened Culture

It is a remote, harsh, unforgiving land in which the Hopi live. Yet this same rugged remoteness has long served to protect them from outside threats. Their culture has been threatened for more than four hundred years—by Spanish soldiers and priests, by American government officials and missionaries and by the more powerful and numerous Navajo who surround them.

For the most part the Hopi have been successful in retaining their cultural identity. For centuries their greatest weapon was their inaccessibility. They were simply

A Hopi woman weaves a blanket outside a hut on the remote, rugged terrain of the Hopi Reservation in Arizona.

so far away that outsiders found it hard to sustain attempts at conquest or conversion.

Technology, however, has shrunk the distance. The outside world is as close as a few hours' drive, a phone call, or an e-mail. The Hopi, except for a few ultratraditionalists, have accepted modern technology, but they recognize that the intrusion of Anglo culture poses a threat to their ancient heritage.

There are other challenges as well. Not only the Hopi way of life but also the land itself is threatened as the dispute with the Navajo continues. The specter of famine no longer lingers over the mesas, but good jobs are scarce and the unemployment and alcoholism rates are high. The survival of the Hopi will depend on their ability to do what they always have done—take the best from what is new and blend it with the traditional to maintain harmony and balance.

Chapter 1

The Emergence

Only since the mid-1900s has there been a written Hopi language. Until then all knowledge—including the stories of how the Hopi came to be—was passed by word of mouth through the generations. It is little wonder, then, that stories of Hopi creation vary widely from clan to clan, from village to village.

Yet all the stories contain a common thread: emergence from an underworld and a long period of wandering before the gathering of the clans at the mesas, the center of the universe. And as with many cultures, ancient tradition and scientific data are reflected in one another.

The Four Worlds

According to Hopi tradition, we live today in the Fourth World. The first was created by Dewa, the sun god, far under the surface of the earth. The only living creatures were insects, which had none of the spiritual qualities desired by Dewa.

Dewa sent his messenger, Spider Woman, to these creatures. She led them to a large cave on a higher level. This was the Second World, and as they reached it the insects became animals. They could not live in harmony and fought with one another, so Dewa again sent Spider Woman, who led the animals to yet another level.

Here, in the Third World, the animals became people. But life was difficult in the Third World. The light was poor, and corn was hard to grow. *Powakas*, or witches, spread discontent among the people, some of whom grew lazy and refused to work. Others came to believe they had created themselves and stopped worshiping Dewa.

Once more, Dewa sent Spider Woman to the people. She told those faithful to Dewa that they should find another place to live, but she did not tell them where they should go.

The chiefs and medicine men decided to seek yet another world above them. They sent for Eagle, strongest of all birds. Eagle agreed to help them. Flying as high

Hopi men in ceremonial costumes hike to a mesa top, circa 1900. According to legend, the Hopi wandered for generations before settling in the mesa region.

as possible, he saw an opening, but was unable to reach it.

Other birds—Hawk, Swallow, and Dove—also tried to help, but none was able to reach the opening in the sky. Finally the people called tiny Shrike, who succeeded in reaching the opening and flew into the Fourth World. There, Shrike found Masauu, god of fire and death. Told of the wishes of the good people of the Third World, Masauu told Shrike he would welcome them to his world to build villages and plant corn.

The Final Obstacle

Shrike returned with the good news, but a problem remained. How were the people to reach the *sipapu*, the opening between worlds? Spider Woman came to their aid once more, sending for Chipmunk, who knew how to make plants grow.

After many plants failed to reach the opening, Chipmunk tried bamboo. The people sang sacred songs and the bamboo grew tall and straight, at last reaching through the *sipapu*. Chipmunk gnawed a hole at the base of the huge bamboo shoot so that the people could climb up the inside.

As the people emerged into the Fourth World, they were greeted by Mockingbird, who assigned each person to a tribe with its own language—the Hopi, Utes, Apache, Navajo, and Zuni as well as the *bahana*, or white people. When Mockingbird finished his song, no more people were allowed to come through the stalk. The *sipapu* was covered with water to hide it. The Hopi believe it was located in the bed of the Little Colorado River about fifty miles west of the mesas.

The Short, Blue Corn

Mockingbird called the tribes together, placing ears of different kinds of corn on the ground. Each tribe was to choose an ear, symbolic of the kind of life it would lead. When the Hopi's turn came there was only one ear left—a stubby ear of blue corn. The Hopi leader picked it up. Their lives would be hard, Mockingbird told them, but they would endure, outlasting all other tribes.

The tribes then departed in different directions to find the lands Mockingbird had assigned to them. At last, only the Hopi and the *bahana* remained. The latter went east, and Hopi tradition says that, some

Shrike and Masauu

When Shrike was finally able to fly through the *sipapu* into the Fourth World, he encountered the god Masauu. Hopi elder Dan Evehema gives his version of their meeting in his book *Hotevilla: Hopi Shrine of the Covenant,* cowritten with Thomas E. Mails.

"The new world was beautiful. The earth was green and in bloom. The bird observed all his instructions. His sense of wisdom guided him to the being he was instructed to seek. When he found him it was high noon, for the being, Masauu, the Great Spirit, was preparing his noonday meal. Ears of corn lay beside the fire. He flew down and lit on top of his *kisi* [shady house] and sounded his arrival. Masauu was not surprised by the visitor, for by his wisdom and sense of smell he already knew someone was coming. Respectfully he welcomed him and invited him to sit down. The interview was brief and to the point. 'Why are you here? Could it be important?' 'Yes,' said Moochnee [Shrike], 'I was sent here by the underworld people. They wish to come to your land and live with you, for their ways have become corrupted. With your permission they wish to move here with you and start a new life. This is why I have come.' Masauu replied bluntly, but with respect, 'They may come.'

With this message the bird returned to the underworld. While he was gone the Kikmongwi [chief] and the leaders had continued to pray for his successful return. Upon his return with the good news of the new world and Masauu's permission for them to come, they were overjoyed."

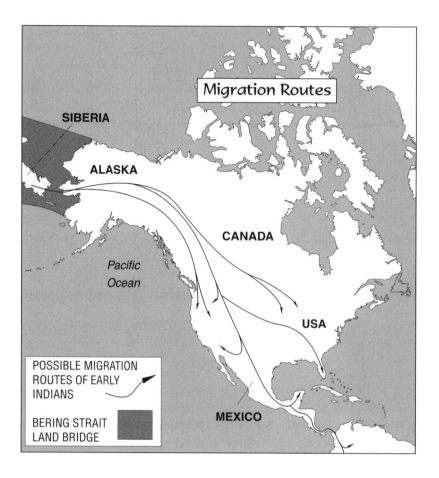

Migration Routes

SIBERIA

ALASKA

CANADA

Pacific
Ocean

USA

POSSIBLE MIGRATION
ROUTES OF EARLY
INDIANS

BERING STRAIT
LAND BRIDGE

MEXICO

day, a *bahana*, or "white brother" will come, bringing peace and prosperity.

Finally, the Hopi set out. Mockingbird told them they would reach their homeland at the center of the universe after many years. They had been chosen, Mockingbird said, to be guardians of this sacred spot. They were to seek "the way," not only to their lands, but also to a way of life in which they were to live in peace and harmony with nature and with all people. Their name was to be *Hopitu-Shimunu*, which can be translated

as "people of peace" or "people of the way."

The Tusqua

The Hopi wandered for generations, dividing into smaller groups, each of which went its own way. At last one group reached the area of the mesas. They saw the dead body of a bear and considered it to be a good omen. The chief decreed that from then on they would be known as the Bear Clan. The Bear Clan settled near the mesas, their crops flourished, and they knew they had found their *tusqua*, or homeland.

The next group to come along saw the same carcass. Needing something with which to carry their belongings, they cut strips of hide from the body and thus became the Bear Strap Clan. A third group saw a bluebird sitting on the carcass and became the Bluebird Clan.

As each new clan arrived, it had to ask permission from the Bear Clan to stay, telling what it would contribute to the good of all Hopi. In some cases it was a new variety of corn, in others a new ceremony. Other clans were experienced potters; some were warriors. The Bow Clan crafted superior weapons.

As the *tusqua* grew, many villages were built. Each contained members of several clans, but the headman of each village, the *kikmongwi,* had to be a member of the Bear Clan. As each new clan arrived, its traditions and ceremonies became part of the fabric of Hopi life. Centuries passed and, except for a rare raid by a neighboring tribe, the people lived in peace, following the Hopi Way.

The Scientific View

The Hopi creation story—emergence from another world, division into tribes, and dispersal—is not unlike the view of modern science about the appearance of humans in North America. The scientific version is that the emergence was across a land bridge that once connected Alaska and Russia across the Bering Sea. This migration is thought to have begun about thirty-five thousand years ago and to have continued intermittently for some twenty thousand years.

Waves of Native American groups crossed into the new world, eventually migrating into every corner. The people from whom the Hopi descended settled in the southwestern part of North America in the Four Corners region—the point where the present-day states of New Mexico, Arizona, Colorado, and Utah meet.

The prehistory of the Hopi and other related tribes is divided into three time periods: the Desert Tradition, Mogollon Tradition, and Anasazi Tradition. Scientists have dated remains found at Desert Tradition campsites as being ten thousand years old. These people, sometimes known as Basketmakers since they had not yet learned to make pottery, were always on the move, gathering edible plants and hunting small animals.

About 3000 B.C. the Basketmakers discovered how to grow corn, which soon became not only the staple of their diet but also the focus—along with rainfall—of their religious ceremonies. A more settled agricultural society developed, with people living in semipermanent homes built under overhanging ledges of rock and farming in nearby valleys. They dug circular pits, lined them with stone, and used them both for storage and to bury their dead. These pits were the forerunners of the kiva, underground ceremonial chambers still used today, powerful symbols of the emergence from a lower world.

The Migration

After the people emerged into the Fourth World, they were formed into groups and sent off to wander until they found their true homelands. This version is found in *Book of the Hopi* by Frank Waters.

"He [the god Masauu] was the first being the people had met here, and they were very respectful to him. 'Will you give us your permission to live on this land?' they asked.

'Yes, I will give you my permission as owner of the land.'

'Will you be our leader?' the people then asked.

'No,' replied Masauu. 'A greater one than I has given you a plan to fulfill first. When the previous parts of the world were pushed underneath the water, this new land was pushed up in the middle to become the backbone of the earth. You are now standing on its *atvila* [west slope]. But you have not yet made your migrations. You have not yet followed your stars to the place where you will meet and settle. This you must do before I can become your leader. But if you go back to evil ways again, I will take over the earth from you, for I am its caretaker, guardian, and protector. To the north you will find cold and ice. That is the Back Door to this land, and those who may come through this Back Door will enter without my consent. So go now and claim the land with my permission.'

When Masauu disappeared, the people divided into groups and clans to begin their migrations."

The Mogollon Tradition

The Mogollon Tradition began about two thousand years ago when the people moved from under their rock shelters and built houses. At first, these were pithouses, circular pits lined with stone walls and covered with roofs of brush and mud. Gradually houses were constructed aboveground, grouped into villages, but the pits were retained for storage and ceremonies. The grouping of houses marked the transition from the Basketmaker period to the Pueblo period, the name coming from the Spanish word for town.

Sometime between A.D. 500 and 700 the Mogollon people developed pottery. Also about this time they began to use the bow and arrow, making it possible to hunt larger game and add more meat to the diet. Houses grew more complex, sometimes made two stories high out of stone blocks with the kiva increasingly used for religious purposes instead of storage and burial. The first villages on the Hopi mesas

A pottery bowl from the Mogollon culture features a drawing depicting childbirth.

even five stories tall. Often, such houses were built in a "U" shape surrounding a courtyard in which was kiva.

The Anasazi dominated the American Southwest from the Rio Grande River to the southern tip of Nevada. There were six main branches, one of which—called the Kayenta from the present-day Navajo town in far northern Arizona—encompassed the ancestors of the Hopi. More villages were established near the mesas, but the major population centers were to the north.

The Anasazi culture flourished for more than two hundred years. Cotton was introduced, and weaving developed into an art. Basketmaking declined, but pottery was much more advanced, particularly among the Hopi, who used coal for firing the pots instead of wood. The higher temperature produced a lustrous yellow finish much admired throughout the Southwest.

The Anasazi traded pottery, blankets, and other goods with other peoples as far away as the coast of California and the interior of Mexico. They particularly prized parrots and other tropical birds from Mexico, using their brilliant tail feathers for ceremonial dress.

date from this period, and those who lived there can be called the first true Hopi.

The Anasazi Tradition

The Anasazi Tradition began in about A.D. 1100. The word itself is Navajo and means "ancient enemies." The Hopi prefer to use the term *Hisatsinom*, or "our ancestors," but Anasazi has become such a common term that most Hopi employ it. The Anasazi built large villages holding a thousand or more residents and featuring large "apartment houses" two, three, and

Architectural Changes

As architecture grew more complex, the kiva underwent a change. Instead of a round chamber, it became square and later rectangular. It was now used exclusively for religious purposes as a place to keep ceremonial items and to conduct secret rites. The kiva was for the exclusive use of a clan, whose members plastered and re-plastered the walls, painting them with sacred symbols that changed with the passing generations.

Sometime about A.D. 1340, however, the climate in the Four Corners area changed.

Severe droughts dried up the streams the Anasazi depended on for irrigating their fields. Also, scientists speculate, new, war-like people may have pressured the Anasazi from the north. For whatever reason, the Anasazi abandoned their population centers, moving south and east.

The drought and resulting population shift dramatically changed the Hopi *tusqua.* Of the forty-six small villages, all but eleven were abandoned. Those that

A village of multistoried cliff dwellings from the Anasazi Tradition has been reconstructed and preserved at Mesa Verde National Park in Colorado.

The Founding of Orabi

Orabi, on Third Mesa, is the oldest continuously inhabited town in North America. This description of its founding about A.D. 1150 is found in *Hotevilla: Hopi Shrine of the Covenant* by Thomas E. Mails and Dan Evehema.

"The village of Orabi was settled and built in accordance with the instructions of the Great Spirit. The Bow Clan chief was the father of the ceremonial order. They remained under the leadership of the Bow Clan for some time, perhaps until corruptions set in. . . .

Later the Bear Clan took over. This might have been because the bear is strong and mighty. There may have been other reasons too, such as a prophecy which told that a bear, sleeping somewhere in the northern part of what is now called Europe, would awaken at a certain time and walk to the northern part of this country where he would wait. This group is called Bear Clan because they came across a dead bear at the place of the shield symbol. Most of the important people claimed to be of the Bear Clan, including the Bluebird and Spider Clan people.

For some reason the Coyote Clan, who migrated from Shgotkee near Walpi, were considered bad people, though very clever. At first they were not permitted to enter but, in accord with our custom, on the fourth request they were admitted, on agreement that they would act as a protection and in time speak for the chief should difficulties arise. But they were warned to be cautious, though faithful ones might remain true to the last. So it is with all clans, for along the way most of us will deceive our leaders for glory, which will tend to pollute our ways and jeopardize our beliefs."

The village of Orabi during the late nineteenth century.

remained grew larger in population, and three more were established. The migrations from the north continued, clan after clan arriving just as in the Hopi creation story. They gathered in villages atop and below the mesas, growing crops, evolving into an ever more complex society, and seeking harmony with the world around them. Their world would be forever changed in the mid-1500s when it was intruded on by visitors from yet another world—one the Hopi could scarcely have imagined.

Chapter 2

The Hopi Way

The traditional Hopi—and the majority fall in that category—are perhaps the most religious people on earth. Religion is not merely a part of their life, it *is* their life, governing every aspect of how they live and think. Walter Hough, in his book about the Hopi written in 1915, said, "If we could pick the threads of religion from the warp and woof [fabric] of Hopi life there apparently would not be much left."[1] Much has changed in the world around the Hopi since that was written, but their inner world is the same as it has been for centuries—a constant search and striving for balance and harmony with all things.

Hopi religious practices extend far beyond what is normal in modern American society, where formal worship is often confined to a short period of time one day per week. Even the five daily prayers required of devout Muslims cannot match the Hopi "way." To the Hopi, every waking action, no matter how simple or routine, and every thought are integral parts of a universe in which all things are bound together in a grand pattern: the Hopi Way.

A World of Spirits

The Hopi believe that all things not only were made by Co-tuk-inung-wa, the great creator god, but that they were given individual spirits. Thus, while human beings have inner spirits or "souls," so also do animals, rocks, trees, water, clouds, and every other object. All these *sina*, or spirits, are part of the Hopi Way, the pattern of harmony set forth at the creation by the gods.

Animals and inanimate objects are seen to fulfill their roles automatically, not having been given a spiritual nature and the power of choice by the gods. Humans, on the other hand, particularly the Hopi, have the responsibility of seeking always to act and think in such a way as to maintain the divine pattern. It is thus up to the Hopi to honor the gods both physically by carrying out the various rites and ceremonies, and spiritually by maintaining a "good

Hopi men engage in a religious ceremony using corn and prayer sticks. Religion dominates every aspect of Hopi life.

heart," harmony within themselves and with all other things. So it is that religion has been infused into Hopi life to include even the most ordinary of daily tasks.

Because humans have been given freedom of choice by the gods, all do not follow the Way. Such people, including the small percentage who have become Christians, are called *ka-Hopi*, or "not Hopi," by those Hopi who follow the Way. Even worse are the people who acknowledge the Hopi Way but actively work against it, trying to disrupt the balance of nature. Such people are called *powakas*—"two hearts" or witches—who dedicate them-

selves to evil. Although traditional Hopi acknowledge that some of their own misfortunes, such as disease, can be attributed to their failure to follow the Way, some occasionally suspect that they have been bewitched.

The Hopi Gods

In following the Way, the Hopi are following the instruction of the gods. There are many gods—as opposed to spirits—in Hopi tradition, but seven are major gods. Co-tuk-inung-wa, the creator of all things, stands above the others. Closely related to Co-tuk-inung-wa are Muingwa, god of germination and guardian of life, and Gna-tum-si, creator of life.

Dewa, the sun god who is also known as the "father" because he watches over the world, is next in importance to Co-tuk-inung-wa. Masauu, god of death and fire, controls all change. Baho-li-konga, the serpent god, controls earthly moisture, including blood, plant sap, and water. Omau is the god of clouds and rain.

The Hopi do not pray directly to their gods. Instead, they use intermediaries, much as many Christians pray to saints to intercede with God on their behalf. In the Hopi's case, these intermediaries are called *katsina*, or "respected spirit," most frequently spelled "kachina." Kachinas are not gods, but spirits. Many represent the spirits that the Hopi believe inhabit every object and thus outwardly resemble eagles, turtles, wolves, coal, stars, and so on. They also may represent Hopi ancestors or the basic forces of life. Their names may be translatable and refer to a physical feature, such as Longhair, Left-handed, Blue Face. Still others have no English translation.

Kachina Dance

The best-known figure of Hopi culture is the kachina, the spirit represented in ceremonies by a masked dancer. With their beautiful costumes and elaborate masks, the kachinas move in solemn time to the hypnotic chant and beat of drum. This description is from *Hopi,* by Susanne and Jack Page.

"Abruptly, and in synchrony with the drum, the kachinas begin a low, mournful, and rhythmic chant, a deep bass, and they began to dance, stamping their moccasined feet on the ground and moving their hands alternately up and down, the rattles' sound adding to the slight offbeat of the turtle shells and sleigh bells. The sun beat down as the long line of kachinas chanted and moved slowly, first in one direction, then in the other, an occasional hesitation step interrupting their steady stomping. The white-haired man moved up and down the line, sprinkling the kachinas with cornmeal as if, by that gesture, he were feeding them, and he called out occasional instructions. The audience was silent and still; the only sounds were the insistent boom of the drum, heard above the Aeolian [sighing] chant of the kachinas and the clacking of turtle shells and the jangle of sleigh bells. After several minutes, the drum stopped, as did the chant, with a descending *oooooaaaw* and the hiss of a single rattle. There was a fragment of silence and suddenly the line of dancers began another chant: the plaza was filled with their single voice, the people riveted by their pounding rhythm and the thunder of the drum."

There are more than three hundred kachinas, but the exact number cannot be determined. Some, because a clan dies out or a ceremony falls into disuse, become extinct and new ones come into being. The principal ceremonies feature about thirty major kachinas, but the number may vary from village to village.

Hopi believe that the kachinas live in the San Francisco Mountains that loom on the southwestern horizon. They spend roughly half the year, however, with the Hopi, and their presence is reflected in the kachina dances. In these dances, men dress in elaborate costumes and masks. The dancers strive, through prayer and keeping a good heart, to be not just an imi-tator of a kachina, but to actually become a physical form of the kachina spirit itself.

Throughout the dances and the associated ceremonies, the Hopi pray to the kachinas and make offerings to them. They believe that if they perform the ceremonials properly and reverently, the kachinas will take their prayers to the gods, who will reward them with plentiful rain and bountiful crops.

The Kiva

The kachina masks, costumes, and all the objects used in the ceremonies are stored in the kiva, or "world below," the sacred chamber that evolved from the ancient round pithouses into rectangular, com-

Costumed kachina dancers circle Orabi plaza during a Hopi harvest dance in the early twentieth century.

pletely or at least mostly underground chambers. The men descend into the kiva on ladders through a trapdoor. Directly under the trapdoor is a fire pit, next to which is a circular hole symbolizing the *sipapu* through which humans emerged into the Fourth World. The ladder represents the bamboo reed through which they climbed. Only those who have been initiated into a secret society may enter the kiva belonging to that society.

Hopi Snake priests descend into a kiva for a ceremony.

The kachina ceremonies are part of a ceremonial calendar built around the eternal cycle of the seasons. The ceremonies have different emphases, but all center on the rebirth of the earth after winter and on the planting, nourishing and growing of the crops necessary—at least in ancient times—for survival. Not every ceremony is conducted each year. Not all are held at the same time every year or in all villages but instead at times when the head priest of the clan that "owns" the ceremony in that village thinks the time is right.

The Ceremonial Year

The ceremonial year begins in mid-November with *Wuwuchim*, whose focus is the germination of life. It lasts sixteen days, eight days of preparation and eight days of ceremonies, ending with a public dance. After the kindling of a fire symbolizing the creation of life, runners from the Two-Horn Society carry burning branches to the *Wuchim*, Flute, and One-Horn kivas. In all four kivas boys are then initiated into the respective societies with a series of rituals, the last of which includes a drenching with cold water, symbolically washing away sins in much the same way as with Christian baptism.

The next major ceremony, *Soyal*, or "all year," celebrates the first appearance of life after its germination. Lasting twenty days in its full form, it is conducted around the winter solstice in December, the shortest day of the year. After eight

Wuwuchim Ceremony

The most solemn Hopi ceremonies are carried out in subterranean kivas and seldom described to outsiders. This description of part of the *Wuwuchim* ceremony by a chief of the Two-Horn Society is found in *Book of the Hopi* by Frank Waters.

"'Early next morning,' he related, 'I, the Two Horn chief, pick up my *mongko* [chief's stick, a symbol of authority] and my *chòchmingwu* [Corn Mother figure] and I go to the Wuchim Kiva. I enter in silence, for all the men inside are in deep concentration, all heads bowed, not a face looking up. I stand at the right of the ladder, not stepping down to the lower level. There I remain. It is my time to speak. I have the authority. If there is any movement of heads toward me or around the kiva it is an indication of disrespect to me and our faith.

'My first command is, "Go now to your homes and bring the food in, and when you have prepared the ceremonial meal, sing praises to the food and make a joyous sound with your voice and your feet and your actions."

'When the meal is finished and the food taken away, my next command is, "Go out and cut the willows and bring in the eagle plumes with this one thought: that in all your preparations the greatest faith may be carried throughout the world by your harmonious actions. Then you shall watch Our Father the Sun, and when he enters the midpoint of day you shall emerge from your kivas to bless the people of the village with your song and ceremony. Carry the ceremony as far as you can till sundown."'"

days of preparation the first kachina of the year, the *Soyal* kachina makes his appearance, carrying four *pahos*, or prayer sticks, that he buries at the entrance to the principal kiva.

A series of ceremonies then takes place, led by members of the five participating clans. Finally, the four *pahos* are dug up and given to kachinas who in turn bury each at a kiva that will be involved in the next great ceremony, *Powamu*, in February.

Powamu, or "put in order," completes the series of ceremonies signaling the preparation of the earth for growing. It is also known as the "coming in of the kachinas," for it is now that most of these spirits make their appearance.

Powamu

An important part of *Powamu* is the ritual planting of beans in pots. On about the eighth day after planting, the first sprouts appear, signifying the end of winter. On the fifteenth day the elaborate Bean Dance is conducted, the many kachinas dancing in their brilliant costumes.

During every fourth *Powamu* Hopi children are initiated into the Kachina Society or the *Powamu* Society. This occurs when the children are between six and nine years of age. Ceremonial mothers and fathers will have chosen which societies the children will enter, and the children have been taught the function of the society and duties of the members. The ceremonies conclude when frightening kachinas called *Hu*, or "whippers," lash the bare legs,

backs, and buttocks of the new members with branches from yucca plants. Finally, the kachinas remove their masks, and the children recognize them as relatives and neighbors.

Through the spring and early summer the kachinas dance virtually every weekend in the plaza of at least one village. Though not among the more important ceremonies, these dances are religious in nature, asking the gods—as always—to send rain and a good harvest.

Hopi Clowns

Even though they have religious purposes, the kachina dances are by no means completely solemn. The *koyew*, or clowns, see to that. Their bodies painted with horizontal black and white bands, they entertain the audience during times when the kachinas are not present. Demonstrating the Hopi's broad sense of humor and ability to laugh at themselves, the clowns perform exaggerated parodies of the kachinas. Their bawdy antics are also directed at members of the audience, especially outsiders who have come to watch the ceremony.

Orabi villagers perch on pueblos to view a Hopi ceremonial dance. At far right is a Hopi clown, his body painted with horizontal black and white bands.

The kachina season ends with the *Niman*, or "going home," ceremony that begins with the summer solstice on June 21. Following secret ceremonies inside the kivas, the *Niman* dance, one of the most beautiful of all the Hopi rites, is conducted. It begins at sunrise and ends at sunset, when the kachinas silently file out of the village and disappear down the mesa, their spirits returning to their home in the far-off mountains.

Even though the kachinas have gone, the ceremonial year is far from over. Two major rites, performed in August of alternating years, are the Flute Ceremony and the Snake-Antelope Ceremony. The Flute Ceremony is outwardly very simple. A procession headed by two young girls winds through the village, periodically tossing small rings on designs drawn in cornmeal on the ground. The rings symbolize the Hopi emergence, and the object of the ceremony is to help bring summer rains.

The Snake Dance

The Snake-Antelope Ceremony, on the other hand, is the most spectacular and best known of all Hopi rituals. Especially famous is the Snake Dance, once condemned as barbaric by missionaries and government officials who tried unsuccessfully to ban it. Members of the Snake Clan dance holding snakes, including poisonous rattlers, in their mouths and hands. As the

A crowd of spectators view the most famous of the Hopi ceremonies, the Snake Dance.

The Snake Dance

The most famous, most photographed of all the Hopi ceremonies is the Snake Dance conducted every other August. Although outsiders are no longer permitted to view the dance, this description of one held in the 1940s is found in *Masked Gods* by Frank Waters.

"And now it begins—what the crowd has been waiting for. A Snake [priest] stoops down into the *kisi* [shelter] and emerges with a snake in his mouth. He holds it gently but firmly between his teeth, just below the head. It is a rattlesnake. The flat bird-like head with its unmoving eyes flattened against his cheek, its spangled body dangling like a long thick cord. Immediately another Snake steps up beside him, a little behind, stroking the rattlesnake with his snake whip with intense concentration. Up and down they commence dancing, while another Snake emerges with a giant bull snake between his teeth. At the end of the circle the Snake dancer gently drops his snake upon the ground and goes after another. The snake raises its sensitive head, darts out its small tongue like antennae, then wriggles like lightning towards the massed spectators. Now the yells and screams and scramble! But a third man, the snake watcher, is waiting. He rushes up. Deftly he grabs the escaping snake, waves the long undulating body over his head, and carries it to the Antelopes [priests]. They smooth it with their feathers and lay it down on a circle of cornmeal."

Snake Dance priests deftly hold poisonous snakes in their mouths and hands.

dancer moves rhythmically around the plaza, he is assisted by another clan member who strokes the snake to keep it calm.

Toward the end of the dance, all the snakes are carried away from the village to the north, south, east, and west. They then slither away into the desert, carrying the Hopi prayers to the gods.

The last three major Hopi ceremonies, *Lakon, Marawu*, and *Owaqlt,* are conducted in September and October, each by a women's society, and symbolize the coming to maturity of the crops. *Lakon* and *Marawu* celebrate the crops coming to maturity. *Owaqlt* signifies that the crops have matured and are ready for the harvest. All three women's ceremonies contain a great deal of sexual symbolism as well as that connected to the crops. With the harvest, the cycle of life has come full circle and must begin anew.

The Eternal Cycle

With the end of *Owaqlt*, the ceremonial year ends. Life has been created and has germinated. The kachinas have lived with the Hopi and their presence has brought rain and allowed the crops to grow. The prayers for rain have continued with the Flute or Snake-Antelope Ceremonies, and the maturing of the crops and the harvest have been marked by *Lakon, Marawu*, and *Owaqlt*. To the Hopi, however, the ceremonial year really has no beginning or end. It is an eternal cycle through which the people, the land, and the gods are bound together.

Although only members of certain societies participate in specific ceremonies, all Hopi feel obligated to attend. Indeed, nonparticipants form an important part of all the public ceremonies, showing respect for the spirits and adding their prayers to those of the dancers and singers. Hopi author Dan Evehema estimates that a traditional Hopi may spend all or part of as many as two hundred days per year attending or participating in ceremonies. This makes it very difficult to hold a job that requires regular attendance. To maintain their traditions—honoring the gods and keeping the Way—in an increasingly fast-paced and nontraditional world is one of the Hopi's greatest challenges.

Chapter 3

Life on the Mesas

While religious observances take an extraordinary amount of the Hopi's time, they still are intended to provide a framework—although a very large one—for everyday life. Not only the ceremonial cycle, but the ordinary patterns of birth, childhood, marriage, work, and death have continued in a distinctively Hopi fashion. They have changed as the world around the mesas has changed, yet remain much the same as in the centuries before the coming of outside influences.

The Clan

The focal point of Hopi society was and still is the clan. The tradition is that after the Emergence, each group was accompanied by a *sowuhti*, a very old, very wise woman to whom the group would turn for guidance. From these *sowuhtim*, then, evolved the Hopi clans that eventually reached the mesas.

Some clans have died out over the centuries, but there are presently thirty-four, each tracing its origins to a female ancestor. Each clan is known by its *wuya*, or symbol. Many have animal names—Bear, Coyote, and Lizard, for instance. Others have taken the names of plants such as Pumpkin and Reed. Still others are named for objects like Cloud, Fog, and Sun. The clans are grouped mainly for ceremonial reasons into what sociologists call phratries. The Parrot Clan, for instance, is the head clan of a phratry that includes the Crow, Rabbit, and Tobacco Clans.

The clans are matriarchal. That is, people are members through the female line. Children automatically become members of their mother's clan. Furthermore, the clans are matrilocal, meaning that when a man marries, he goes to live with his bride's family. He still, however, remains a member of his mother's clan. Marriage between members of the same clan is forbidden.

One family within each clan is considered the one most directly descended from the founder, and the senior woman in that family is the clan mother, the final source

Members of various clans gather to watch an autumn harvest dance. Hopi society is divided into matriarchal clans; children are born into their mother's clan.

for decisions on clan affairs. The clan mother's eldest brother is also very important, organizing the clan's special ceremonies.

Clans are economic as well as social units. Clans, not individuals, own land. The clan mother distributes small plots of land among families, trying to see that the best land is allotted fairly. The boundaries of these pieces of land are marked with painted stones.

Clan families normally live together in large houses with several additions. Over the decades, however, some houses have run out of room, and families built new houses or even moved to other villages. A Hopi away from his or her own home can always be assured of a warm welcome from clan members in other villages. In addition, people in financial or other difficulties can look to their clan members for assistance.

Childhood

Clan members are just as much a part of a Hopi's family as the mother and father. This relationship starts at birth when the child and mother are cared for by the mother's female relatives. Newborn children are washed and bound to a cradle board where they may spend the next six months to a year.

After the first bath the baby is tended by the father's female relatives. Both the mother and baby remain inside the house for twenty days, the curtains drawn tight to keep any sunlight away from the child. At the end of that time the baby is ceremo-nially carried outside at dawn to meet the sun and be named. Most Hopi, in addition to their traditional names, are given common *bahana* names by which they are known to outsiders.

Discipline of very young Hopi children is almost nonexistent. From the time they can walk infants are allowed to do pretty

A Hopi Doctor

Although they have a modern hospital with trained doctors and up-to-date equipment, many Hopi prefer to first consult a traditional healer. This description of a treatment is from *The Hopis: Portrait of a Desert People* by Walter Collins O'Kane.

"To'chi quietly watched the sick woman. Stretched out on an improvised bed, she was restless, turning from one side to the other. Her dark skin was flushed. Clearly she was running a fever. . . . In To'chi's box of medicines there was one that was always good for fever. He could take care of that condition. Then he could set to work on the next measure the patient needed. He emptied the grounds from the coffeepot, rinsed it, poured a cupful of water into it, and placed it on the stove. From his box he took a paper bag containing a supply of dried leaves, brownish in color and faintly aromatic. He placed a handful of these in an empty pan. When the water was boiling he poured it over the leaves, stirring them with a twig. After waiting ten or fifteen minutes, he drained the infusion into a clean cup. He held this to the woman's lips and had her drink half of the contents.

'You'll feel better after you drink this,' he assured her and smiled when she shuddered at the bitter taste. As he knew by experience, the bitterness was no disadvantage. If it had no more taste than water, it would seem to have no power to effect a cure. Two hours later, he gave her the remaining contents of the cup and was encouraged to note that she seemed to be somewhat less restless and to have less fever. . . .

For three days, To'chi maintained his vigil, usually sitting near the sick woman. Twice he changed to a different medicine, and twice he increased the strength of the dark one that he was administering. . . . On the following morning . . . the restlessness of sickness had given way to that of a person who would soon be eager to be up and about."

Young Hopi children are given a great deal of freedom and are seldom disciplined.

much as they please. Even later when they begin taking on responsibilities within the family, punishment is rare because children are firmly taught that misbehavior is against the Hopi Way and causes disharmony. When children must be punished, it is usually by their mother's brothers. Children who seriously misbehave may be visited by ogre kachinas and whipped with yucca branches.

Before the coming of the Europeans and Americans, the Hopi never had schools as such. Children received religious instruction from relatives and began to learn the household and occupational chores that would be their responsibilities as adults. The Spanish and Americans later tried to force education on Hopi children,

sometimes with disastrous results. The Hopi now operate their own schools, including the reservation's first high school, which opened at Kykotsmovi below Third Mesa in 1939 and moved to a modern facility near Keams Canyon in 1989.

Although children are initiated into Kachina or *Powamu* societies while still of elementary school age, they become eligible at about sixteen to join one or more of the secret societies. For a boy, this initiation, at which he is given a secret name by the society, marks his passage into manhood. In addition to joining societies, girls go through a four-day corn-grinding ceremony, after which they are considered women, ready to begin the complicated series of courtship and wedding rituals.

Marriage

Traditional Hopi weddings are long, drawn-out ceremonies often requiring years to complete. Usually, young men conduct a rabbit hunt soon after the corn-grinding ceremony, inviting the women who had taken part. The women take cornmeal cakes, each giving extras to a man in whom she is especially interested. A short time later she will grind corn somewhere in her house where she can be seen from outside. If the man comes to visit her there—not entering the house, but talking through the window or door—the courtship has officially begun.

If all goes well, the woman will take the cornbread known as "piki" to the man's home. If he eats it, the couple are officially engaged. The woman and her female relatives then begin to grind great amounts of corn for the wedding feast. At the same time, the man and his male relatives begin weaving robes for the bride. There will be two similar robes, one for the marriage and one in which the woman will be buried after she dies. For the groom, the bride's female relatives weave a *ha-hawpi*, a wedding basket. The basket, like the bride's second dress, will eventually be part of the man's funeral. The close connection between weddings and funerals shows that all Hopi are expected to marry.

When the corn and the baskets to carry it in are ready, the woman moves to the man's house for four days, grinding corn under the supervision of his mother. On the fourth day the actual ceremony is begun. The groom's mother washes the hair of the bride, and the bride's mother washes the hair of the groom. Then the bride and her relatives prepare a wedding breakfast and a feast for that evening.

Days later, when the bride's robes have been finished, the groom's father sprinkles

A Hopi woman holds a traditional wedding basket, a tray woven for the groom by a bride's family.

Ceremony Before Marriage

Part of the lengthy Hopi wedding formalities involves ceremonial washing of hair, symbolically washing away the frivolities of youth. Don Talayesva describes his own marriage in this passage from *Sun Chief*, edited by Leo W. Simmons.

"When I entered the house, I saw many eyes staring at me. There were Irene's mother and her sisters, Blanche's mother and her relatives, in fact all the women of the Fire Clan, also the women of the Coyote and Water-Coyote clans, and most of my . . . aunts. They had assembled to give me a bath. My mother was assisting Irene's mother with the yucca suds. I was so timid that I took steps not more than an inch long. My mother said, 'Hurry up.' I laid back my shirt collar and knelt with Irene before a bowl of yucca suds. My relatives washed Irene's head and her relatives washed mine. Then they poured all the suds into one bowl, put our heads together, mixed our hair and twisted it into one strand to unite us for life."

cornmeal in a path back to her home. The bride, now in her white cotton robe with a colorful sash, returns to her house but without her new husband. Over the next few days or weeks the bride and her relatives grind still more corn, carrying it to the groom's house to "pay" his family. When the man has been paid for he moves to the bride's home to live with her family.

The actual ceremony, which can be completed in a matter of weeks, sometimes drags out for years. The baskets for the corn and the traditionally woven wedding garments are very expensive. The bride and groom's families sometimes have to save for months, even years, before the ceremony can proceed. This is not as much of a hardship as it appears, since most couples also go through a civil ceremony and live as man and wife as the traditional rituals proceed.

Modern Courtship

As with many things on the Hopi reservation, traditional courtship has a modern counterpart. Anglo-style romances bloom in the high school, including conversations and hand-holding in the halls and at school dances. Young men and women participate in social dances in the villages, but they are highly structured and involve little or no physical contact. A couple strolling together hand in hand through a village would be frowned on by their elders.

Men and women have different traditionally prescribed tasks within the clan, although some of the ancient distinctions have been blurred by modern influences. For example, the making of baskets and pottery was originally, but is not now, the exclusive task of women. And among the Hopi, as in other cultures, women cared for the homes and the children and did all the cooking.

An important part of every girl's education is learning to make piki, which remains a favorite food. The woman places a flat stone, also called a piki, on an open fire. When it is hot she spreads cottonseed oil on the surface and then, with her hands, spreads on a wafer-thin layer of cornmeal,

most often made from blue corn. When the piki has baked, it is peeled off the stone and either rolled or folded. Rather bland in taste, piki is served as an accompaniment to main dishes such as mutton stew.

Men were in charge of planting and tending the crops, caring for livestock, and hunting game. They also had responsibility for defending the village and played the most important roles—as they still do—in religious ceremonies. Another traditional male occupation was weaving. Men would gather in the kivas, spinning wool and cotton and weaving blankets and other clothing. Hopi weaving, however, is

Hopi girls in the late nineteenth century grind corn to make piki (see loaves at center). Learning to prepare this favorite Hopi food is an important part of a young girl's education.

almost a lost art. Except in ceremonies, virtually all Hopi wear the same clothing to be found anywhere else.

Agriculture

Until the twentieth century the Hopi economy was exclusively agricultural. When the crops were bountiful, the people prospered. When the rains did not come and the crops failed, many starved. Over the centuries the Hopi developed different techniques of dryland farming. Some crops are planted in areas near "washes," or creek beds, that overflow after a rainstorm, spreading water over the fields. Other planting is done in sand dunes that are outwardly dry but moist below the surface.

Hopi farmers plant corn a foot deep in these dunes and have developed strains with deep roots and short stalks that can withstand the winds that sweep the mesa country. Corn remains the principal crop and the staple of the Hopi diet. Its importance is reflected in the language, which has fifteen words to describe different kinds of corn and cornmeal.

A Hopi man carries a bundle of dried, harvested corn on his back. Corn is the main staple of the Hopi diet.

Home Construction

The Hopi traditionally build their own houses, to the greatest extent possible with only the help of friends and relatives. It is an extension of centuries of living off the land. This account is from *The Hopis: Portrait of a Desert People* by Walter Collins O'Kane.

"When a man sets out to build a house, he is not concerned with the wage scales that have been established by carpenters' or plasterers' unions. Some one may help him with the building, but, if so, it will be a member of his own family or a neighbor with whom he strikes up a trade. Quite likely, he will do the entire job himself. His building materials he will get largely from the desert, with the addition of some items which he must buy. He is not interested in the price of Portland cement because he can make his own excellent mortar out of clay and sand, both of which he knows just where to find, and this mortar will serve well in laying up his well-built stone walls. He needs no package material from a store for the inside finish of his walls, because another native clay deposit can supply that."

Other principal food crops are beans, squash, and pumpkins, while cotton is cultivated to make cloth. The Spanish introduced other crops such as melons, peaches, apricots, onions and chili peppers.

Livestock raising, although it is growing, has never been as important to the Hopi as to some of their neighbors, such as the Navajo. Water for large flocks is scarce, and the Hopi have preferred to stay close to their villages rather than range far and wide in search of pasture land. Overgrazing the lands close to the mesas eventually led to a U.S. government order to limit the number of sheep, but mutton remains a popular dish.

Trees in the Hopi lands are few, small, and unsuitable for building. Formerly, men had to make the eighty-mile journey west to the San Francisco Mountains to obtain pine logs for roof beams. Now they buy most building materials from outside the reservation.

Architecture

Outside influences have had less of an influence in Hopi architecture, especially in the older villages, than in other aspects of daily life. While trailer homes and frame houses are found in some of the newer towns at the foot of the mesas, the majority of dwellings follow the ancient pueblo pattern. Houses are multistory and grouped around a central plaza where dances and other ceremonies take place.

Most houses are built of adobe—bricks made of mud and straw—or the native sandstone that is plentiful at the foot of the mesas. Here and there, however, dwellings have been built or repaired with modern cinder blocks, metal window frames have been used in place of brightly painted wood, and modern roofing materials are the rule rather than the exception.

Most houses now have electricity, although the poles and wires look distinctly out of place alongside the ancient houses. Most now also have indoor plumbing, although there are plenty of privies to be seen on the edge of the cliffs. The exception to modernity is at the tiny village of Walpi, perched on the far tip of First Mesa. The most conservative of villages, its residents—only about eight families—have voted to have neither electricity nor plumbing. Music from battery-powered

The few families that remain in the small village of Walpi on the cliffs of First Mesa have chosen to resist modernization and live much as their ancestors did.

radios can be heard as one walks down the narrow dusty street, however.

Government

The right of the people of Walpi to make such a decision is typical of the Hopi style of government. Traditionally, each village is a self-governing unit. The heads of each clan in the village select a leader known as the *kikmongwi*. The *kikmongwi,* who must be a member of the Bear Clan, can give advice but has no absolute power. Rather, he uses his personal influence to try to settle disputes and bring about agreement. Most of his duties are religious rather than political.

When the U.S. government decided in the 1930s that every Native American tribe should have a tribal council with which the government could deal, the Hopi were reluctant. While there is a Hopi Tribal Council theoretically made up of representatives from all the villages, many Hopi do not recognize its authority and protest when it claims to speak for the entire tribe. The council has nevertheless taken on some important projects such as the building of community centers, the development of the Hopi Cultural Center on Second Mesa, and the establishment of an all-Hopi police force.

In any event, the spirit world is more important to the traditional Hopi than any form of government. If people maintain good hearts and are in harmony with all things, they will, after death, be reborn in the underworld as spirits. These spirits take earthly form in clouds and mist. Thus it is the spirits of Hopi ancestors that bring the life-giving rain and so maintain the cycle of life.

Funeral Rites

The transformation of the spirit after death is symbolized by a white cotton mask placed over the face of the deceased at a funeral. Women are dressed in the second of their two white wedding robes and men in distinctively colored blankets. Placed alongside a man is his *hahawpi,* a traylike wedding basket on which his spirit is thought to descend to the underworld. After the funeral ceremony relatives carry the body to the rocky valleys between the mesas, there either to be buried, covered with stones, or placed upright in a crevice. Food is placed next to the grave as an offering, and on the fourth day, so the Hopi believe, the soul is carried away.

With death as throughout life, religion is the cement that holds Hopi existence together. Work and prayer are inextricably connected. As Mischa Titiev, a sociologist who studied the Hopi, said, "Shorn of its elaborate, detailed and colorful superstructure . . . the entire complex of Hopi religious behavior [is] a unified attempt to safeguard Hopi tradition from danger of disintegration and dissolution."[2] That danger, begun with the arrival of the Spanish, continues as the outside world intrudes ever increasingly on that of the Hopi.

Chapter 4

The Spaniards

The harmony of the Hopi's world was violently and permanently disrupted in 1540 when the Spaniards made their first appearance at the mesas. While they would bring many beneficial additions to the Hopi culture such as new crops and more advanced farming methods, they also brought cruelty and greed, leaving behind a lasting distrust of Europeans and, later, Americans.

Rumors of Wealth

Shortly after Spanish adventurers conquered the vast Aztec Empire and established a colonial capital in Mexico City, rumors reached them of fabulous riches in the unexplored lands to the north. It was said that there were seven cities so wealthy the most common utensils were made out of gold. An expedition led by Francisco de Coronado set out in 1540 to find them, but they found instead only the dusty pueblos of the Zuni, about one hundred miles southeast of the Hopi.

Perhaps to rid themselves of these unwelcome visitors, the Zuni told Coronado that the seven cities he sought lay to the northwest in the area the Spanish later named Tusayan. Coronado dispatched a lieutenant, Pedro de Tovar, with a small armed force to investigate. In July he arrived below Antelope Mesa, east of the other three mesas on which Kawaioukuh and other Hopi villages then existed.

After an initial and futile attempt at resistance during which some of the men of Kawaioukuh were run down by horses, which they had never before seen, the leaders submitted to the newcomers and presented them with gifts. According to the official account of Coronado's expedition, "The people of the whole district came together that day and submitted themselves, and they allowed him [Tovar] to enter their villages to visit, buy, sell and barter with them."[3]

The Spanish received food, cloth, and animal skins, but what they really wanted—gold, silver, and turquoise—was nowhere to be found. Disappointed, Tovar soon returned to report his lack of success

A painting depicts the expedition of Francisco de Coronado, which set out in 1540 with hopes of finding vast riches in the unexplored lands north of Mexico.

to Coronado, but he brought back another rumor. The Hopi had told him of a great river north of the Hopi homeland. Coronado sent another officer, Garcia Lopez de Cardenas, to find it, which he did with the help of Hopi guides.

When Cardenas arrived at the river, he and his men thought—viewing it from the canyon rim above—that it was only about six feet wide, although the Hopi claimed it was more than a mile across. When they descended into the canyon, the Spaniards discovered to their amazement that the Hopi were correct. Moreover, boulders, which from above seemed about the height of a man, "were bigger than the great tower of Seville."[4] The Hopi had just

provided Europeans their first view of the Grand Canyon.

The Oñate Expedition

The next major Spanish expedition to the Tusayan was more serious than those before it because the goal was colonization instead of mere plunder. In 1597 Juan de Oñate led more than 400 men, 130 accompanied by their families, north to the Rio Grande River. There, on April 30, he formally took possession of "all the kingdoms and provinces of [the region the Spaniards called] New Mexico"[5] in the name of the king of Spain. Pressing north along the river, he established outposts, forcing the native peoples to dig

Nonresistance

Often, when faced with an obviously superior Spanish armed force, the Hopi adopted a policy of nonresistance. In 1692 Don Diego de Vargas led troops to the mesas as part of a campaign to reconquer what Spain had lost as a result of the Pueblo Revolt. At first the Hopi made as if to resist, then thought better of it. As related in a 1693 account of the expedition, found in *Pages from Hopi History* by Harry C. James, the Hopi of the village of Awatobi

"laid down their arms and knelt on the ground. After this the Spaniards went on to the pueblo and entered what served as a public square . . . and there they took possession of the town in the name of the king and our Lord. . . . He [Vargas] ordered them to bring some firewood, because it was very cold, and, noting that they appeared sullen, he threatened them that the fire would be built with their own weapons and even their own bodies. . . . They brought him a great deal of wood. . . . When the chief, Miguel, asked the General to act as godfather to his grandchildren and had received this favor, which he prized highly, he begged the Spanish governor to honor him again by being his guest."

fortifications and taking from them by force whatever was needed.

The Hopi were too far away from Oñate's base of operations along the Rio Grande River in New Mexico to be directly affected. Their only contact came in November when Oñate visited the mesas, where he was accepted peacefully by what he called the "Mohoqui, or Mohoce."[6] This is the earliest reference to the name by which the Hopi would be known for centuries by most of the outside world. Usually spelled Moqui, it is thought to have been a term of insult begun by the Zuni from their word *A'mukwi*, or "dead ones."

The Franciscans

The Hopi's isolation came to an end in 1629 when Spanish missionaries, priests of the Franciscan order, intensified efforts to convert the Native Americans to Christianity. Conversion, however, did not mean that the Hopi would be equal with the Spaniards. Indeed, they were to be virtual slaves, forced to build churches and forts and supply the Europeans with food.

On August 20, 1629, three missionaries—Francisco Porras, Andreas Gutierrez, and Cristobal de la Concepcion—arrived at Awatobi on Antelope Mesa. They announced plans to build a mission church in honor of San Bernardino, whose feast day it was. The Hopi, who doubtless had heard of Spanish harshness at the pueblos to the east, were so hostile that the priests had to be accompanied by soldiers everywhere they went.

Porras, head of the mission, made little headway in converting the Hopi until the native priests challenged him to show the power of Christianity. They brought to him a young boy who had been blind since birth. According to an account written later by another priest, Alonso de Benavides, Porras placed a cross on the eyes of the boy, whereupon he was able to see. Then, Benavides wrote, "The Indians were so stunned and convinced that they venerated the father [Porras] as a saint and promised to believe what he taught them. They took the boy in their arms and carried him through the streets and plazas, proclaiming that all should become Christians and do as the father taught them, for it was the truth and their own priests were deceiving imposters."[7]

This apparent miracle opened the way for construction to begin on churches, not

Hopi guides provided the Spaniards with their first glimpse of the awe-inspiring Grand Canyon.

The remains of an abandoned church on the Hopi Reservation are a reminder of Christian missionaries' failed efforts to convert the Hopi.

only at Awatobi, but also at Orabi (San Francisco) and Shongopovi (San Bartolomé). The Hopi furnished the labor, and hard labor it was. The enormous roof beams had to be dragged across the sandstone, leaving marks that are still visible. Even in the twentieth century, the long-abandoned church at Orabi was known as the "slave church."

The Franciscans wanted not only to establish their own religion but also to stamp out that of the Hopi. They deliberately built the Awatobi church on top of an important kiva. They banned Hopi rituals and destroyed sacred objects.

Economic Hardship

The Spanish brought economic hardship as well. They appropriated native land and forced the Hopi to work on it, but used the crops for themselves and sometimes sold any surplus to the Spanish government. It was little wonder that Hopi hostility flamed anew. When Porras died in 1663 his fellow priests were convinced he had been poisoned.

The harsh treatment continued. In 1655 one priest, Salvador de Guerra, caught an Orabi man worshiping in the traditional manner. According to an official report of a hearing in the colonial capital of Santa

Fe, the priest lashed the man until he was "bathed in blood"[8] then poured turpentine on him and set him afire. Similar incidents were reported throughout New Mexico, and the pueblo tribes grew more and more bitter, finally erupting in the great rebellion of 1680.

The leader of the Pueblo Revolt was a religious leader named Popé from San Juan, north of Santa Fe. He spent years organizing the uprising and getting the support of other pueblos. He sent runners across the Southwest carrying messages painted on buckskin. He set a date of August 13 and sent a knotted cord to each pueblo so the days could be counted off.

Word of the revolt leaked out, however, and Popé ordered it to begin on August 10. The Rio Grande pueblos launched a coordinated attack, and the Spaniards were either killed or took refuge in the governor's palace in Santa Fe. Five days later, realizing their situation was hopeless, the Spaniards broke through the besiegers and fled.

The Hopi Uprising

The uprising of the Hopi probably took place a few days later than that along the Rio Grande but was just as well planned and executed. Spanish records list the leader as Francisco de Espeleta, a Hopi who had taken a Spanish name. Tradition in Orabi says that the revolt there was led by two men, Haneena and Chavayo.

At dawn, men wearing kachina masks attacked and killed the soldiers guarding the mission churches, then broke into the churches and killed the priests. At least four priests—two at Orabi, one at Awatobi, and one at Shongopovi—died, their bodies either thrown from the edge of the mesas or buried under the rocks below.

The victorious Hopi then set out to destroy every trace of Spanish occupation. They sealed the church bells and soldiers' armor in caves and destroyed the church buildings, using the stones and wood for their own buildings. They gave the soldiers' pikes and spears to the One-Horn Society for use in ceremonies.

The Pueblo Revolt had three lasting effects on the Hopi. First, to be better prepared for invasion they knew would follow, they moved some of their villages from below the mesas to the tops. Walpi, Mishongnovi, and Shongopovi were moved to higher ground, where they have remained ever since. Others, like Shipolovi, were newly established high above the plain.

Second, Tusayan shortly would become a home for refugees fleeing from New Mexico once the Spanish reconquest began. Several groups, in keeping with Hopi tradition, requested permission from the Bear Clan to remain. Most eventually moved back to their own lands, but one large group, the Tewa, founded the village of Hano on First Mesa and remain there still, maintaining a separate identity although they have often intermarried with the Hopi.

Third, and most important, the Pueblo Revolt marked the end of the Spanish occupation of Tusayan. A few Spanish

Men pose on steps leading up to the village of Shipolovi. To be better prepared in the event of an invasion, the Hopi moved or established new villages high above the plain.

expeditions ventured forth over the next decades, but none was strong enough to reestablish what had been lost. In 1692 Diego de Vargas led an armed company to return the Hopi to Spanish rule. Faced with a superior force, the Hopi allowed priests accompanying Vargas to baptize many people, but Vargas and the priests stayed only a few days and most of those who had been baptized soon returned to the Hopi Way.

The Destruction of Awatobi

In 1700 two Franciscans were determined to win the Hopi back to Christianity. They were met by a sizeable and hostile force led by Espeleta, who, although he threatened the priests, did not want to make the mistake of killing them and thus attracting Spanish revenge. He allowed them to reconvert many villagers at Awatobi and then to return to New Mexico to prepare for the reestablishment of the mission of San Bernardino.

When the Spaniards departed, the Hopi took action. The *kikmongwi* of Awatobi, Tapolo, was disturbed that so many of his people had accepted Christianity, far more than anywhere else in Tusayan. He determined to stamp out this foreign religion and enlisted the help of the men of Walpi, Shongopovi, Mishongnovi, and Orabi to help him.

Using some excuse, Tapolo got most of the men of Awatobi to gather inside a large kiva, having warned non-Christians to stay away. When they had descended the lad-der, he gave the signal for attack, and the men of the other villages swept into the town. They pulled the ladder from the kiva entrance, trapping those inside. They then threw burning bundles of firewood and chili peppers down the entrance to suffo-cate their enemies. They ran through the town killing most of the remaining men and rounding up the women and children.

The survivors were taken to a spot, still known as Maschomo, or Skeleton Mound, where a dispute broke out about what was to be done with the captives. Many, in-cluding all the able-bodied men and boys, were slaughtered, and the women and

Aftermath of Revolt

Even as they retreated from New Mexico after the Pueblo Revolt of 1680, the Spanish predicted that the victorious Native Americans would soon be fighting one another. They were correct. This description, written by a Franciscan missionary, is found in *Pages from Hopi History* by Harry C. James.

"The rebel pueblos began to quarrel and wage bitter war. The Queres, Taos, and Pecos fought against the Tehuas and Tanos; and the latter deposed Popé . . . electing Luis Tupatú in his place. He ruled the Tehuas and Tanos till 1688, when Popé was again elected; but died soon, and Tu-patú was again chosen. . . . Later, each pueblo of the Queres governed itself. The Apaches were at peace with some of the pueblos, but in others did all the damage they could. The Yutas [Ute], as soon as they learned the misfortunes of the Spanish waged ceaseless war on the Jémez, Taos, and Picuries, and especially the Tehuas on whom they committed great ravages. Not only thus and with civil wars were the apostates [the pueblo rebels] afflicted, but also with hunger and pestilence . . . of the Tiguas only a few families escaped and retired to the province of Aloqui [the Hopi]; of the Piros, none escaped."

young children were distributed among the four villages.

The next day the conquerors returned to Awatobi. They were satisfied only when they had set fire to the houses, smashed pottery and weaving looms, and left the village a complete ruin. Awatobi was the last Hopi village on Antelope Mesa, but its rituals endured, taken to other villages by the few survivors.

The destruction of Awatobi is perhaps the most dramatic event in Hopi history as well as the most important. It signaled the end of the Spanish attempt to convert the Hopi, whose religious practices then went largely undisturbed for more than a century. By the time other missionaries—this time from the United States—came to Tusayan, the Hopi Way was so solidly reentrenched as to be able to resist all attempts to dislodge it. At the start of the twenty-first century, despite strenuous attempts at conversion, about 95 percent of the Hopi follow their traditional beliefs.

Spanish Influence Declines

Contacts between the Hopi and Spaniards in the 1700s were infrequent. Few had consequences of any significance. A military expedition in 1716 ended after only

Sand-covered rock formations are all that remain of the village of Awatobi, which was destroyed by the Spanish in 1700.

A Recommendation

Because of their peaceful nature and the fact that they were very remote from the centers of Spanish influence, the Hopi took few active roles in the periodic revolts of the pueblo people against the Spaniards. Yet, their willingness to harbor refugees resulted in this recommendation from Don Bernardo Miera in 1776. It is found in *Pages from Hopi History* by Harry C. James.

"These Moquis, for many reasons . . . should be brought down by force from their cliffs. I will say only that even though they do not make war, they are obnoxious to New Mexico, for they serve as an asylum for the many apostates [rebels] from the Christian pueblos of that province. On the other hand, they are Indians who are very highly civilized, much given to labor, and not addicted to idleness. For this reason, although they live in that sterile region, they lack nothing in the way of food and clothing, and their houses are built of stone and mortar and are two or three stories high. . . . They live on the tops of those high and steep mesas in six separate pueblos. But they could come down from them without the shedding of blood, with only the threat of a siege . . . by a company of soldiers stationed at the waterholes which they have at the foot of the cliffs, and in less than a week they would surrender and be ready to do whatever might be required of them."

one short skirmish. In the late 1770s Spanish explorers came through Tusayan while trying to find a new route between Santa Fe and Monterey, California. The expedition's leader, Silvestre de Escalante, tried to convince Hopi leaders to send a delegation to Santa Fe to sign an agreement guaranteeing the safety of a route through Hopi lands, but they refused.

The final years of Spanish rule of the American Southwest were tragic ones for the Hopi. Diseases introduced by the Europeans reached epidemic proportions. Hundreds died of smallpox and of measles.

In addition, the rains failed for three years in a row starting in 1777. The crops died, and the Hopi starved. The governor of New Mexico, Juan de Anza, went to Tusayan in person to try to help. He offered food that the Hopi, true to their tradition, refused because they had nothing to give in return. De Anza put the Hopi population at 798, whereas Escalante only five years before had given a figure of 7,494.

As if all this were not enough, the Navajo began to increase their raids on Hopi territory. Spain had reconquered the

The Hopi became famous for their beautiful blankets woven from the wool of sheep.

Rio Grande area and had, with the help of the pueblo tribes, defeated Navajo raiders. A treaty between Spain and the Navajo in 1819 caused the Navajo to look west to the Hopi instead of east.

Spanish Rule Ends

Spanish rule ended two years later when a revolution established the Republic of Mexico. It left behind a mixed legacy for the Hopi. They were better off in many ways, especially economically. Their diet, which had been confined mainly to corn, squash, beans, and what meat small game could provide, was improved with the addition of new crops and the raising of livestock for beef and mutton. The sheep also provided wool, and the Hopi became famous for their blankets.

The Spanish also provided the Hopi with farming implements, metal tools, and—indirectly—with firearms that made them better hunters. The Hopi used Spanish trade routes to sell their pottery, weaving, and other goods far and wide, bringing back many previously unknown items to Tusayan.

On the other hand, the Spanish had brought physical cruelty and had made the Hopi slaves in all but name. They had tried to eradicate traditional beliefs and rituals. They had also brought previously unknown diseases. Some, like measles, were devastating to the Hopi, who unlike the Spaniards had not built up immunity over generations.

The Spanish also left behind a deep distrust of Europeans. Hopi legends told of a *bahana,* a white brother who would bring peace and prosperity. At first their elders thought this savior might be among the Spaniards. They found out differently, and their distrust was carried over to those *bahana* who followed the Spaniards.

Chapter 5

The Americans

Twenty-five years after the Spanish flag was lowered over New Mexico, the banner of the United States was raised. The intervening years were filled with violence and disorder, but when their new rulers were at last in power, the Hopi found to their sorrow that they were little better off than before.

The Hopi got a warning that the Americans would not provide their sought-after *bahana* as early as 1834 when a group of about forty explorers and trappers led by U.S. Army captain Joseph Walker plundered their fields. When the Hopi men protested, twenty of them were shot.

Such events were all too common. The young Republic of Mexico had enough troubles close to home. It could spare little effort toward keeping order in far-off Tusayan. As a result, the peace-loving Hopi suffered repeated raids by the Apache, Ute and, ever increasingly, by the Navajo. Also, Mexican bandits preyed upon the countryside, kidnapping women and children to be sold as slaves.

The American Takeover

The United States declared war on Mexico in 1846 and General Stephen Kearney and a small force was dispatched to Santa Fe. So great was the lawlessness that it was almost with a sense of relief that Mexican authorities and settlers in Santa Fe welcomed him. Virtually everyone—Mexicans and Indians, farmers and merchants—thought the *norteamericanos* would bring peace and prosperity. So without a shot having been fired, the vast American Southwest—including the Hopi—were suddenly part of the United States Territory of New Mexico.

The takeover had little immediate impact on the Hopi. The first Indian agent, James S. Calhoun, was appointed in 1849, but the situation was still so dangerous that he never ventured far from Santa Fe. He was genuinely interested in the welfare of the Native Americans and tried his best to better their lot, but could get little support from Washington.

included Ute, Zuni, and Hopi. The Hopi, representing all villages except Orabi, which had a profound distrust of all foreigners, were used primarily as scouts and guides, having little talent for warfare.

After a cruel and bitter campaign, Carson's army defeated the Navajo, who were marched away in captivity on the "Long Walk" to Fort Sumner, New Mexico. Finally there was some peace, but little prosperity. The Hopi crops had been poor, the winter of 1863–1864 was unusually harsh, and many Hopi fields had been destroyed in the mistaken belief they belonged to the Navajo.

Despite the defeat of the Navajo it was not until 1869 that a government agency was established for the Hopi. Even then, it was at Fort Wingate, far to the east of the mesas. It moved closer—to Fort Defiance—in 1871, and in 1873 an outpost was established at Keams Canyon, only about ten miles east of First Mesa, where the agency remains today.

In 1863 Colonel Christopher "Kit" Carson recruited the Hopi and other tribes to help defeat the Navajo.

Return of the Navajo

The Hopi's lands were soon threatened again. The Navajo, released from captivity, began to graze their flocks ever closer to the mesas. Mormon settlers from Utah established a settlement near the Hopi vil-

The Navajo raids on Hopi, Zuni, and the Rio Grande pueblos grew so bold and frequent that the U.S. Army finally decided to step in. In 1863 Colonel Christopher "Kit" Carson, the famous scout and Indian fighter, assembled an army of regular soldiers and volunteers. The volunteers

lage of Moencopi, forty miles west of Third Mesa. A railroad was nearing completion to the south that would make it easier for American ranchers and merchants to settle nearby.

Government agents to the Hopi were worried enough to encourage Washington to set aside a reservation. The government agreed, and on December 16, 1882, President Chester A. Arthur issued an executive order setting aside 2.5 million acres "for the use and occupancy of the Moqui and other such Indians as the Secretary of the Interior may see fit to settle thereon."[9] The phrase "other such Indians" would be the cause of much controversy in future years.

No one consulted the Hopi before these lines on a map were drawn. The area did not include large portions of the *tusqua,* which the Hopi considered their ancestral homeland. Many sacred sites such as the San Francisco Mountains and the Grand Canyon were outside the reservation. Furthermore, while the Hopi could use and occupy the land, they did not own it. Control remained with the U.S. government.

Despite the establishment of the reservation, the government paid little attention

The Allotment Plan

In the 1890s the Bureau of Indian Affairs decided that the best way to destroy the Hopi clan system was to introduce private ownership of land through allotments to individuals. Such a program was unworkable for the Hopi, as Acting Agent S.H. Plummer reported, as quoted in *Pages from Hopi History* by Harry C. James.

"No improvement in condition of Hopis during the past year . . . the plan of building houses in the valleys for these Indians, with the view of persuading them to abandon their overcrowded pueblo dwellings on the high mesas, does not seem to be as successful as desired.

Many of the houses built in the valleys are unoccupied the greater portion of the year. Their habits, customs and general mode of living are so intimately connected with the conditions of life on the mesas that it is doubtful whether anything else than compulsion will cause them to abandon their pueblo dwellings. It has been the custom for years for these people to cultivate their lands in common. Owing to the shifting nature of their planting grounds, it would be almost impossible to maintain any allotment to individuals. It is believed that the best interest of the tribe would be promoted by granting the petition [asking for discontinuation of allotments]."

The Keams Canyon Boarding School opened in 1887. Hopi children were required to live at the school and conform to a whole new way of life.

to the Hopi. The Keams Canyon agency was vacated between 1882 and 1887, but then the Americans came to stay. James Gallagher arrived in May and became the first representative of the United States to become a full-time resident of the reservation. In October he opened the first Hopi school.

The School Controversy

Although Hopi leaders had petitioned the government for the new school, it quickly resulted in a controversy that lasted for decades. The opening of the school marked the start of government attempts to force a new way of life on the Hopi and

of the Hopi's determination to resist. The Hopi could not understand why no school was held on Sunday or on Christmas and other religious holidays, but Hopi children were required to attend on village ceremonial days. Village chiefs and clan leaders began to persuade the people to keep their children from school for fear that they would be converted to alien ways.

Tradition was perhaps strongest in Orabi, and when the people there persisted in keeping their children from school, Superintendent Ralph Collins brought in troops from Fort Defiance. On December 28, 1890, they entered Orabi and forcibly rounded up 104 children—some of whom had been undergoing an initiation ceremony in a kiva—carrying them off to Keams Canyon. They were forced to live there while going to school and were not allowed to visit their homes.

In 1891 government officials decided that if the Hopi were to be "civilized," their social and religious structure, centered around clans and villages, had to be broken up. The method chosen was to convince the Hopi to accept allotments of land—forty acres of farmland and sixty acres of rangeland per adult male. The government reasoned that private ownership of land would replace the system whereby land was held in common by the clan and thus would destroy the clan system.

The Hopi were first perplexed, then amused, and finally alarmed. They protested that the allotment system was not only against their ancient tradition, but also that it made no sense. Different sections of land became more or less fertile each year with shifting sands and varying rainfall. Hopi custom was to plant where crops would grow. To confine a person to a single unchanging parcel of land might mean poverty.

The government would not budge. It sent surveyors to the reservation to mark off the allotments in neat rectangular pieces. The Hopi traditionalists, especially

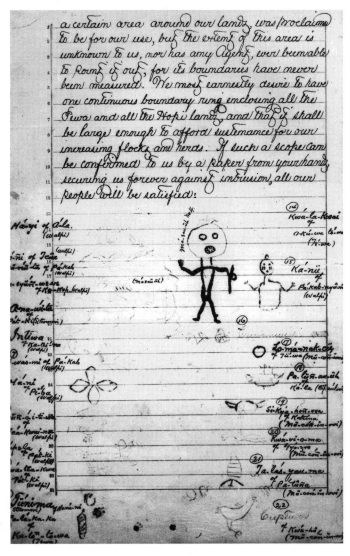

An 1894 petition to the U.S. government from the leaders of the Hopi tribe requests formal clarification of all Hopi territory.

those at Orabi, fought back by removing the surveyors' stakes at night.

Friendlies and Hostiles

Not all the Hopi refused to learn the white man's ways. Those who sent their children to school and accepted the allotment lands, moving from their villages into new houses built by the government, came to be known as "Friendlies." The conservatives, such as those who interfered with the surveyors, were called "Hostiles."

When the government persisted in the allotment program, the Hostiles took direct action against the Friendlies, trying to drive them away from their fields. Government troops stepped in, arresting nineteen Hostile leaders and shipping them to the federal prison at Alcatraz off the coast of California where they remained for seven months.

The split between Hopi factions deepened. When smallpox broke out in Shongopovi, the Hostiles wanted to forbid government health workers to enter the village to give vaccinations. The Friendlies protested, the government sided with them, and the Hostiles left Shongopovi, taking refuge in Orabi.

The leader of the Friendlies in Orabi was a young chief named Tewaquaptewa. The Hostiles were led by Yokeoma, a bitter opponent of everything to do with the government and its programs. Tension between the groups grew to the extent that it divided clans. Societies built separate kivas and conducted separate ceremonies, something totally counter to Hopi tradition

and inconsistent with the Hopi Way of seeking universal harmony.

In September 1906 Tewaquaptewa and his followers identified the newcomers from Shongopovi as the chief cause of the trouble and determined to drive them from Orabi. Yokeoma and his followers moved to protect their allies. It looked as if a civil war might break out.

Warfare, however, has never been the style of the Hopi. On September 8 Tewaquaptewa and Yokeoma agreed that there would be no bloodshed, but also agreed that one group would have to leave Orabi forever. That afternoon, as the two groups faced one another, Yokeoma drew a line in the dirt with his toe and then walked across it toward the village. If his opponents could push him back over the line, he said, his group would be the one to leave.

Yokeoma and a supporter of Tewaquaptewa named Humihongnewa placed their hands on one another's shoulders. Their followers moved in behind them, each placing his hands on the back of the man in front of him and the push was on. Back and forth they went. Yokeoma at times was lifted completely clear of the crowd before sinking back into it. At last he was pushed back across the line. That night, taking only what they could carry with them, Yokeoma and his followers—some of whom had to be removed by force— went northwest where they founded the village of Hotevilla, still one of the most conservative of Hopi communities.

Today, an inscription on a boulder marks the spot of the conflict at Orabi. Echoing

Eviction from Orabi

In 1906 the division in Orabi between Hopi who welcomed the white man's ways and those opposed to change grew so deep that the "Hostiles," losers of a kind of mass wrestling match, were forced to leave. One of those evicted was a man known as Grandfather Titus. This excerpt from his story is found in *Hotevilla: Hope Shrine of the Covenant* by Thomas E. Mails and Dan Evehema.

"I am telling of my own experience. When we were banished from Orabi in 1906, we were evicted by our own people who co-operated with the government; they were people of our village, who came into our houses and threw us out. They knew our leaders and caught them first. They had no respect and were very rough. One of our men lay down, as if glued to the ground. They could not budge him. They drove us all to the north side of the village. . . . They even bit old people such as Yuki-uma's [Yokeoma's] father, and tore their clothing to pieces. Everyone known as Hostile was evicted. They dragged them by the hair through the dust of the streets to the edge of the village, where the women of the Friendlies were mocking, 'Ha Ha! Get out of here! Go west! Be like the Navajos, who never rest! Don't ever come back! Since you don't want *bahana* things, you don't need to wear their shawls,' and they took away any clothing that had come from white people. All of our women, and we children were chased from our homes, and the doors were bolted."

the words of Yokeoma, it reads, "Well it have to be done this way now that when you pass me over the LINE it will be DONE. September 8, 1906."[10] The Friendlies had won, but Orabi itself was the ultimate loser. Once the largest and proudest village, it continued to decline. At the end of the twentieth century barely one hundred people lived there, and most of its ancient dwellings were tumbledown ruins.

Even worse than the division of Orabi, the conflict had really settled nothing. The rift among the Hopi would continue. The Friendlies and Hostiles of 1906 would become the Progressives and Traditionalists of 2002. The debate would continue over how much of the modern world the Hopi could accept and still remain Hopi.

Burton's Harshness

Most of the government officials who were sent to the Hopi were determined that, like it or not, the Hopi Way would be abandoned for the white man's way. When Charles Burton became the first combination school superintendent and Indian

Once a large and influential Hopi village, Orabi declined and fell into ruins following the conflict of 1906.

agent in 1900, he continued the practice of forcibly rounding up children and virtually imprisoning them in school. Furthermore, he decreed that Hopi men and boys could no longer wear their hair in the traditional shoulder-length style. Some were held down by government workers and Navajo while their hair was cut. Students at the schools were whipped unmercifully for small infractions of the rules.

Unfortunately for Burton, one of the teachers at the school who was sympathetic toward the Hopi was Belle Axtell Kolp, whose uncle had been governor of New Mexico. She resigned her post in protest and wrote a lengthy article for the magazine *Out West* published by Charles Lummis, another person who had taken up the cause of Native Americans. Burton was reprimanded, but managed to keep his job.

The Hopi—as were so many other Native American peoples of the early twentieth century—were governed mainly by men who got their jobs as Indian agents through political connections. Some thought they had the welfare of those under their care at heart, but "welfare" to them meant forcing the Indians to abandon their traditions. Many genuinely sought to better the lives of the Indians, while at the same time despising them for trying to hold on to their way of life.

Such a man was Leo Crane, superintendent and agent to the Hopi from 1911 to 1919. Crane accomplished many positive things on the reservation. School buildings were renovated, and the first hospital was built. Crane saw to it that greater supplies of tools and farming implements came to the Hopi. He planted groves of trees and introduced new breeds of livestock. He even urged that the name of the reservation be changed from Moqui to Hopi.

At the same time, however, Crane had little regard for the Hopi, their villages, and their traditions. Of Tewaquaptewa, he wrote, "I tried for eight long years to make a sensible human being of him, and failed for lack of material."[11] He called Hotevilla "a dirtier duplicate of the other pueblos without their picturesque setting."[12] His strongest language was reserved for those who refused to send their children to school: "The Hopi present so much immorality that an attempt to do more than protect children . . . and round up the most scandalous of the older villagers would project a moral war. . . . They [the Hopi] begin as children to live on a moral plane little above their livestock."[13]

Like many of his predecessors, Crane used brute force to get the Hopi children to school and to keep them there. In December 1911 he led troops into Hotevilla and carried away sixty-nine children to Keams Canyon where they were kept for four years, isolated from their families. When the adults protested they were arrested. Yokeoma and other leaders were repeatedly jailed.

A Teacher's Report

Belle Axtell Kolp, niece of a former governor of New Mexico, caused a furor when she abruptly resigned as a teacher at a Hopi school in 1903. She wrote an account of her experiences for a magazine. This excerpt is found in *Bullying the Moqui* by Charles F. Lummis.

"In my room, which was my living room (as I did my own housekeeping at Orabi), I had many pictures, paintings, and photographs which the schoolchildren took great delight in looking at and asking questions about. It was all new to them, and I enjoyed explaining things. One day, after they had been coming to my room for three or four weeks, Mr. Ballinger [the school superintendent] said to me, 'Don't you know that you are breaking school rules by allowing the schoolchildren to visit you in your room.' . . . Then I asked him if he objected to their visits to me, and if so, why, since they were learning of things outside their little world. His reply was, 'We do not want them to know too much, and they must stay away.' And he gave those orders to the children, with threats of whipping if they disobeyed. I was told of these threats by several of the children, both boys and girls. It must have been so, for they did not come anymore, except to look in the doorway, smile, and shake their heads."

Attempts to force the white man's way on Native Americans are evident in these photographs of Hopi students in 1907 upon entering an Indian school (top), and after one year at the school.

The Bursum Bill

Such agents as Burton and Crane thought they had the best interests of the Hopi at heart. That was not the case, however, among top officials of the Bureau of Indian Affairs in Washington in the early 1920s. The commissioner, Charles Burke, took part in a plan by Secretary of the Interior Albert Fall to pass federal legislation that would take from the Hopi and other pueblo tribes their most valuable lands and give mineral and oil rights to white speculators.

This legislation, known as the Bursum Bill, passed the Senate before most in the

Native American community were aware of its implications. Once they were, the pueblo tribes united for the first time since the Pueblo Revolt of 1680 and were joined by many influential non-Indians. Under the glare of publicity, other scandals in the Department of the Interior came to light. Fall was forced to resign in 1923 and was eventually sent to prison for accepting bribes while in office. The Bursum Bill never became law.

The entire episode focused national attention on how Native Americans had been treated by the government of the United States. In 1927 the Brookings Institution conducted a study and issued a report calling for reform. An investigation and hearings by the U.S. Senate led to the resignation of Burke and his chief deputy.

In 1933 President Franklin D. Roosevelt finally heeded the call, appointing John Collier commissioner of Indian Affairs. Highly knowledgeable and sympathetic, Collier worked for passage in 1934 of the Wheeler-Howard Act, better known as the Indian Reorganization Act.

Reforms in the 1930s

Some called this new law the "Magna Carta of the Indians of the United States," and indeed it represented a dramatic shift in the government's attitude toward Native Americans. It abolished the allotment system, restored some lands, set up a limited

Rounding Up Children

Many times in Hopi history agents of the U.S. government have resorted to force in order to get Hopi children to attend schools. This report was sent to Washington by Agent Leo Crane in 1911. It is found in *Book of the Hopi* by Frank Waters.

"I do not know how many houses there are in Hotevilla, but I crawled into every filthy nook and hole of the place, most of them blind traps, half-underground. And I discovered Hopi children in all sorts of hiding places, and through their fright found them in various conditions of cleanliness. It was not an agreeable job; not the sort of work that a sentimentalist would care for. . . . By midday the wagons had trundled away from Hotevilla with 51 girls and 18 boys . . . nearly all had trachoma [an eye infection]. It was winter, and not one of those children had clothing above rags; some were nude. During the journey of 45 miles to the Agency many ragged garments went to pieces; the blankets provided became very necessary as wrappings before the children reached their destination."

Charles Burke, the commissioner of Indian Affairs, was forced to resign after a 1927 investigation revealed unfair treatment of Native Americans by his department.

Hopi had never had a central government. Each village was independent and was governed more by spiritual than political processes. The notion of a tribal council to speak for all Hopi, along with a deep-seated distrust of Washington, made the Hopi very reluctant to accept the plan. The people were divided, as they had been since the 1880s, between those who wanted to cooperate with the United States and those who clung fast to the old ways.

system of self-government, provided loans for tribes to build and operate schools and hospitals, and called for the preservation of traditional cultures including the freedom of religion that had been enjoyed by other Americans since the 1700s.

The act also allowed each tribe to vote whether or not to be organized under a tribal council, a representative body with which the government could deal. The

The Hopi tradition, growing out of a desire for harmony, is to avoid confrontation. Therefore, when the election to create the Hopi Tribal Council was conducted, most people who were opposed simply refused to participate. Only 755 of the approximately 4,000 eligible voters cast ballots, and the measure passed, 651 to 104. Life would improve for the Hopi because of the Indian Reorganization Act, but the division it caused has remained ever since. And the Hopi's problems, within themselves, with the government, and especially with the Navajo, were by no means solved.

Chapter 6

The Missionaries

Government agents and school superintendents were not the only Americans trying to change the Hopi's way of life. Long before the government took an interest in the people on the mesas, Christian missionaries found their way there. While they accomplished much that was good, their attempts at conversion fueled the division among the Hopi. And in the end, their attempts at leading the Hopi down the "Jesus road" ended mostly in failure.

The Mormons

First to arrive were from the Church of Jesus Christ of Latter-day Saints, or the Mormons, as they are usually known. Mormon leader Brigham Young, who had led members of his church to settle in Utah in 1847, was intensely interested in converting Native Americans. The Mormons thought Indians were descendants of the Lost Tribes of Israel and had migrated to North America from Palestine about 600 B.C.

According to the Book of Mormon, the ancestors of the Native Americans forsook the Jewish religion and became "Lamanites," cursed with a dark skin. If they could be converted to Christianity, Young believed, they might become "a white and delightsome people."[14]

Young focused on the Hopi because he had heard they were a peaceful and settled people. He hoped to convince them to move their villages north of the Colorado River and become a buffer between Mormon settlements and more hostile tribes. In 1858 he instructed Jacob Hamblin to leave his farm in southern Utah and carry the proposal to the Hopi.

Hamblin and his group reached Orabi in September. They were greeted in peace. Some Hopi thought the legendary *bahana* deliverer might be among them. The group spent a few weeks learning about the lives and traditions of their Hopi hosts, then Hamblin returned to Utah to report to Young. Four Mormons stayed behind "to study their language, get acquainted with them, and, as they are of the blood of Israel, offer them the gospel."[15]

When the Hopi learned that the Mormons wanted them to abandon their villages and move to the north, they became less friendly. Religious leaders now said these were not the looked-for "white brothers." The Hopi grew so hostile that the four Mormons left and returned to Utah.

Hamblin Returns

Young was persistent. Hamblin visited the Hopi again in 1859, leaving behind two of his men—Marion Shelton and Thales Haskell—to study the people and attempt to win them over to Christianity.

The Mormon missionaries went about their task far differently than had the Spaniards. They treated the Hopi as equals, living with them. They showed genuine interest in ceremonials. They helped build and repair houses and did other work around the villages. Shelton even made a crude fiddle, whose music delighted the Hopi. But, although the Hopi loved to hear the Mormon hymns, they had little interest in abandoning either their homes or their ceremonies.

Shelton and Haskell returned to Utah the next spring, and two years passed before another Mormon mission reached the Hopi. Again, it was led by Hamblin. The group arrived at Orabi in December 1862 and found the Hopi in the middle of a famine. There had been little rain for two years, and forty-six people had died of starvation in the village. The Mormons helped every way they could. Not only did they share their own limited provisions, but they also participated in the ceremonies asking the gods to end

Mormon leader Brigham Young was passionate in his desire to convert the Hopi.

The Hopi village of Moencopi. Despite the establishment of a Mormon settlement near Moencopi in 1879, the Mormons ultimately failed to win converts among the Hopi.

the drought, adding their prayers to those of the Hopi.

The Hopi Visit Utah

Leaving three missionaries behind, Hamblin returned to Utah. He was accompanied by three Hopi men whom he had convinced to come with him to meet Young and other Mormon leaders. When they arrived in Salt Lake City, the Hopi were treated with great respect. Young renewed his request for the entire tribe to settle north of the Colorado River and said he would send a hundred missionaries to help. Mormon scholars questioned the men closely, hoping to find evidence of a link between the Hopi and the ancient tribes of Israel.

Hamblin made several more journeys to the Hopi, but he was never able to con-vince leaders to consider moving north. He was, however, instrumental in the establishment of a new village. He convinced one of the leaders at Orabi, Tuuvi, to lead some families to settle at Moencopi, west of the mesas, in 1870.

Hamblin and Tuuvi became good friends, and the Hopi leader accepted an invitation to travel to Salt Lake City to meet Young. Tuuvi was impressed with the Mormon leader and agreed to provide land near Moencopi for a Mormon settlement. So it was that in 1879 fourteen Mormon families shortly thereafter established the town of Tuba City, which Hamblin named for Tuuvi.

Moencopi is unlike the other Hopi villages in that water from springs is relatively plentiful. Using the streams for irrigation, the Mormons introduced important crops such as wheat, safflower, and turban squash, which still is called "Mormon pumpkin" by the Hopi.

For all their hard work and good works, however, the Mormons failed to win religious converts among the Hopi. In fact, the establishment of Tuba City rekindled the hostility of Hopi leaders, who were afraid their lands would soon be overrun by the newcomers. The U.S. government was also hostile to the Mormons, not so much from concern about the Hopi as from opposition to the Mormon religion, which taught at that time that men could have multiple wives. About the same time as the Hopi Reservation was created, the area around Tuba City and Moencopi was added to the Navajo Reservation. Under pressure from the government, the Mormons sold their farms around Tuba City in 1904 and moved elsewhere. Today only one small Mormon church remains on the reservation.

The Mennonites

At about the same time the Mormon influence was declining, another missionary brought his brand of Christianity to the Hopi. Born in Russia to German parents, Heinrich R. Voth, a member of the Mennonite sect, visited the mesas in 1892. He

Mennonite missionary Heinrich Voth was disgusted yet fascinated by Hopi ceremonies like the Snake Dance (pictured).

Challenging H.R. Voth

According to many accounts, Mennonite missionary Heinrich Voth was an intimidating figure, forcing his way into secret ceremonies in order to add to his store of knowledge about the Hopi. In this passage from his autobiography *Sun Chief,* Don Talayesva described a time he stood up to Voth.

"When I heard that he [Voth] was in my mother's house I went over and told him to get out. I said, 'You break the command-ments of your own God. He has ordered you never to steal or to have any other gods before him. He has told you to avoid all graven images; but you have stolen ours and set them up in your museum. This makes you a thief and an idolator who can never go to heaven.' I knew the Hopi Cloud People despised this man, and even though he was now old and wore a long beard, I had a strong desire to seize him by the collar and kick him off the mesa."

returned a year later with his wife to establish a mission.

Voth was a stern man who exhibited little of the compassion that had marked his Mormon predecessors. Although he was determined to eradicate the Hopi religion, he was nevertheless fascinated by it. But where the Mormons had been invited to witness kiva ceremonies after working alongside the Hopi and earning their trust, Voth simply barged in. On one occasion he simply shoved aside a priest of the Two-Horn Society in order to enter. One elder remembered that Voth "always pushed to the front, anywhere he wanted to be, even in the kivas. Nobody could stop him."[16]

Many aspects of Hopi ceremonies disgusted Voth. He tried to get the government to outlaw the whipping of children at initiations and the more vulgar antics of the clowns at kachina dances. At the same time, however, he was busy learning and recording every part of every ceremony and collecting kachina masks and other sacred objects.

Word of Voth's studies eventually reached Chicago's Field Columbian Museum, which contained one of the country's most outstanding collections of Native American artifacts. The museum's curator, G.A. Dorsey, made two visits to Voth and persuaded him to sell his collection to the museum. The price was five thousand dollars, five times Voth's missionary salary.

The sale caused some controversy in the Mennonite church and on the reservation. Voth was reprimanded by the chairman of the Mennonite Mission Board for paying too much attention to collection and not enough to conversion. Thomas

Keam, who had established a trading post at Antelope Mesa in 1870 and for whom Keams Canyon is named, said, "His sole mission appeared to be that of trading; as he accumulated more in his capacity as a missionary in that time, than I as a licensed trader."[17]

Voth left the Hopi and spent almost two years in Chicago arranging his collection and writing reports of his observations. He was permitted to return to the reservation in 1901 to train a new missionary, but his wife died giving birth the next year and he left for good in 1902.

Few Hopi realized the extent of Voth's collecting and research. Some who visited the Chicago museum years later were dismayed by the reproduction of kiva altars and the detailed description of the most secret ceremonies. Although Voth's work caused a lingering distrust of scientists, it did have some positive effects. Decades after his death, Hopi priests sometimes had to consult Voth's writing for ceremonial details that otherwise would have been lost.

Lack of Progress

The Mennonite mission continued after Voth's departure, but it was very slow work. Although the Mennonites, who had been persecuted in Europe because of their steadfast refusal to serve in the military, appealed to the Hopi's peaceful inclinations, few would leave the Hopi Way. The first Hopi baptism took place in 1909. In

A Missionary's Trials

While the Hopi may have questioned his methods, Heinrich Voth seems to have cared for the Hopi and shared the hard life of the mesa. This excerpt from his notes is found in *Pages from Hopi History* by Harry C. James.

"Our work was essentially a pioneer work, and my dear wife and myself were practically alone to do it. Many times villages on other mesas were visited, very many visits to families were made. Many sick people were looked after and treated. . . . On May 3, 1901, a little daughter was born to us and on May 6 the Lord, who always knows best, took my devoted wife, who so bravely stood by me in all our trials, labors, adversities. . . . We buried her the following day near the station. A few government employees, my sister and some Indians were present. When the men filled the grave little Esther, about 2½ years old, tore herself from my hand, rushed to the nearly filled grave and began to scratch the sand back, crying, 'Those men must not put so much sand on Mama.'"

Despite little success in converting the Hopi, Christian missionaries have persisted in their efforts, as is evidenced by this church built in Moencopi in 1975.

1926, thirty years after the mission began, only fifty-two Hopi had been converted on Third Mesa. By 1950 the number was only ninety-seven.

Voth had begun the first Mennonite church on the reservation at Orabi in 1901. Although it was not completed until after the missionary left, the Hopi always referred to it as the "Voth church." They considered it unlucky. First, as originally planned, it would have blocked the traditional pathway of the kachina. The Mennonites changed the location, but the Hopi apparently had been told by Voth that the building would be a sort of hospital and were angry when they learned it was used almost exclusively for Christian services.

The presence of the church in Orabi has been cited as one of the reasons for the division between the Friendlies and Hostiles that led to the expulsion of one of the groups in 1906. When the church was struck by lightning and destroyed in 1912, some Hopi leaders said it was the will of the gods. The people considered it bewitched and, as with the ruins of the old Spanish mission of San Francisco, refused to go near it.

Despite the lack of conversions, the Mennonites have persisted in their work on the Hopi Reservation, and today there are Mennonite churches at Moencopi and Bakavi as well as at Kykotsmovi, or "New Orabi" below the mesa from the ancient village. Only the church at Kykotsmovi,

Saving a Baby

Some Hopi believed that when a mother died in childbirth and the baby lived, the baby was an evil spirit and thus should be buried alive with the mother. In 1908 Mennonite missionary Mary Schirmer was determined to intervene the next time this happened. The incident is related in *The Vision and the Reality* by Lois Barrett.

"He [the father] said, 'I told all of my sisters asking them to take care of the baby but none of them go near him. They are afraid of him. He is a nice pretty boy; I do not feel like killing him. He is lying on the floor. Nobody has taken care of him since he arrived.' . . . So Miss Schirmer went home to Hotevilla on horseback . . . went to the house and walked in. Two Hopi women were then already busy in the house preparing the baby boy for burial. The heathen naming ceremony which is usually carried out the twentieth day of a child was carried out that morning. . . . They named him *Siwinainiwa* [which] means 'young cedar sprout.' Miss Schirmer waited until they were through with their ceremony and then went and took the baby, wrapped him in a blanket she had brought with her."

The missionary woman adopted the Hopi baby, renaming him Daniel Schirmer. He later became a Mennonite mission worker among his own people and the Cheyenne in Montana.

which is independent of the Mission Board, has more than a few members.

The Baptists

Shortly after the Mennonites began their work at Third Mesa, another denomination started its missionary work with the Hopi on Second Mesa. But, whereas the Mormon and Mennonite leaders had been men, the Baptist effort was exclusively female, at least for the first few years.

An organization known as the National Indian Association had established a mission at Second Mesa in 1894. In six years, however, it failed to convert a single Hopi and the association was ready to turn the mission over to another group. At about the same time, some Christianized Kiowa in Oklahoma sent money to the Women's Baptist Home Mission Society, asking that it be used with another tribe.

So it was that in 1900 Mary G. Burdette of the society made the trip to Second Mesa accompanied only by a Hopi driver who spoke no English. When she arrived at the mission site, it was high noon and the sun was shining brightly. Burdette immediately named the spot "Sunlight Mission" and said that it would light the way for Hopi who remained unconverted.

Some Hopi were ready to listen to her message. Crops had been poor for four years, and the people were hungry. Burdette was convinced the Hopi could be converted and within two years had persuaded the Mission Society to send three other women to work among the Hopi. They held services in a government school in Polacca, which had been established by the U.S. government below First Mesa, until a separate church was built in 1909.

The Baptist women used various methods to entice the Hopi to come to church services. They would make sure that food was available. They had a good organ, powered by the turning of a crank. The Hopi loved both the music and turning the crank.

The Baptists, however, made no compromise with the Hopi ceremonies and traditions. Whereas the Mormons had added their prayers to those of the Hopi and Mennonite Voth had carefully studied their rites, the Baptists told the Hopi that their traditions amounted to idol worship and were an affront to God and Jesus. This aroused the anger of Hopi priests, who began to do everything they could to prevent the people from the First Mesa villages from coming down to Polacca to attend church.

The missionaries decided that if the people would not come to church, they would take church to the people. On Sundays they climbed the mesa to hold services inside people's houses. The Hopi were too polite to forbid them to enter, but the missionaries eventually noticed that, as the service went on, the people would gradually drift away, leaving perhaps only one elderly deaf person as a congregation.

In 1910 a Baptist minister, Lee Thayer, arrived in Keams Canyon. He took over as minister of the Baptist church and also did missionary work among the Navajo. The Baptist mission continued its work through the subsequent years but like the others, with only limited success. A tiny Baptist church—still called Sunlight Mission—holds services at Second Mesa and there is also a small church at Polacca.

Reasons for Failure

The Christian missionaries failed to convert the Hopi for some of the same reasons as the Spanish priests before them. Despite the passage of the centuries and the passage of the railroad through Arizona, the Hopi were still far from the mainstream of American culture. Only the very dedicated could endure the journey to the mesas or the hard life there.

Also, the missionaries were dealing with a different kind of Native American people in the Hopi than elsewhere. Most of their work had been among people who had been uprooted from their ancestral lands or who were traditionally nomadic. The Hopi had been settled for centuries, and their ceremonies and rituals were well established. As Voth wrote,

Mormon leader Joseph Smith preaches to a Native American tribe. The Hopi proved far more resistant to conversion than most other tribes.

been destroyed and lost in their migrations and wars. Among the Hopi the various religious organizations were more intact yet. The same ceremonies they held hundreds of years ago were essentially the same.[18]

Another factor that worked against the Christian missionaries was that they often could not agree among themselves. The Hopi had many societies that worked in harmony to worship the gods and follow the Hopi Way. They could not understand the denominational or interdenominational squabbles among the Christians. In 1953 a Mennonite missionary, Elizabeth White, wrote, "The Hopi, whom we consider spiritually lost, is more quietly spiritually secured today than our missionaries in their confusion of gossip over creed and doctrinal split differences."[19]

The religious conditions were very different. The religious systems among [other tribes] . . . were more or less disintegrated, much of their religious paraphernalia [objects] had

As far back as the migration of the clans it had been the Hopi tradition to learn from newcomers. The Hopi learned much from the missionaries. They planted new crops, learned new farming techniques, studied English at mission schools. They embraced, however, only the things they thought beneficial. The Christian religion was not among them.

Chapter 7

The Navajo

Confrontation with the white man has not been the Hopi's most persistent problem—directly, at least. The Spanish came and went. The American government abandoned its harsh treatment and its policy of trying to stamp out centuries of tradition. Missionaries have concentrated more on helping the people than in turning them aside from the Hopi Way. The one problem, however, that still defies solution after more than four hundred years is that presented by the Navajo.

The Hopi have remained small in numbers. There are about 11,700 Hopi, of whom about 9,000 live on the reservation. The Navajo numbered 225,298 in the 1990 census, with 107,543 living in Arizona and completely surrounding the Hopi. Their relationship has been one of constant tension, the Navajo seeking to expand onto Hopi lands and the Hopi trying to keep them off.

Early Contacts

The Navajo were relative latecomers. One of the Athabascan family of Native Ameri-

cans, they migrated from Canada, reaching the Southwest sometime around A.D. 1200. They made contact with the Hopi during the mid-1500s, and there was trouble between the two peoples almost from the start. Formed by a more aggressive culture, the Navajo soon had a reputation among the Hopi as thieves of corn and livestock. This reputation has endured to a point where Hopi Roy Albert said, "There is a saying in Hopi: When you shake hands with a Navajo, be careful, because his other hand might be reaching for your pocket."[20]

As the Navajo grew more numerous, Hopi stories go, they turned from theft by stealth to open raids in force. Shortly after the Pueblo Revolt, open warfare broke out between the Hopi and the Navajo, and the Hopi began calling the Navajo the *Tasavuhta*, or "pounders," because they sometimes killed enemies by hitting them on the head with a stone ax.

An uneasy peace existed between the Hopi and Navajo in the 1700s. The Navajo did not live in villages but moved

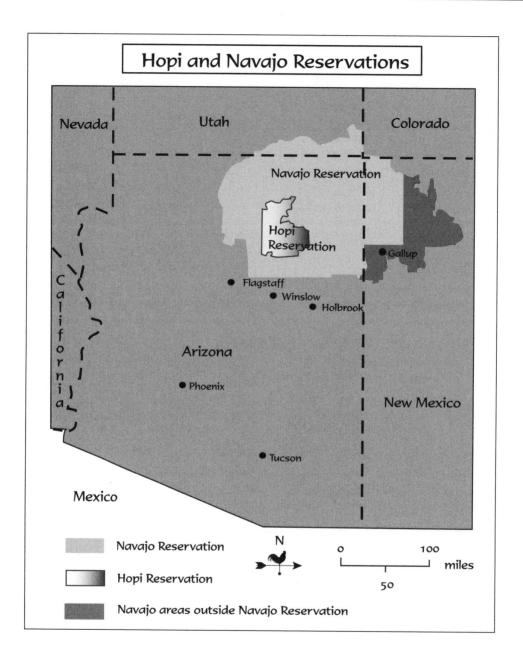

Hopi and Navajo Reservations

Nevada

Utah

Colorado

Navajo Reservation

Hopi Reservation

● Gallup

California

● Flagstaff

● Winslow

● Holbrook

Arizona

● Phoenix

New Mexico

● Tucson

Mexico

Navajo Reservation

Hopi Reservation

Navajo areas outside Navajo Reservation

N

0   100
miles
50

from place to place with their flocks of sheep according to grazing conditions. They had a lively trade with the Hopi, exchanging mutton and wool for corn, beans, fruit, piki, and woven goods. The Hopi, however, were always watchful, afraid that the Navajo would steal what they did not trade for.

Bad feelings between the Hopi and Navajo increased as the latter moved west from New Mexico under pressure from the Spaniards. They increased still more after 1821 when the Mexican government was unable to protect the Hopi from Navajo raids. Eventually, Navajo plundering of the Hopi and other tribes reached a point where the U.S. Army took action against them. Defeated after a cruel campaign and exiled to central New Mexico, the Navajo nursed an enduring bitterness against the Hopi who had been among the army's allies.

A Navajo family in New Mexico in 1873. The Hopi have been in constant conflict with the Navajo for more than four hundred years.

Upon their release from captivity in 1868, the Navajo went to live on a reservation established for them in northeastern Arizona and northwestern New Mexico. The tribe grew and the reservation was expanded westward in 1878 and again in 1880. Soon the Hopi were complaining that the Navajo were not only stealing from their fields, but were also herding their flocks closer to the mesas, stripping the pasture and threatening the water supply.

The Hopi Reservation was not established until 1882, by which time about sixteen hundred Navajo were already living in the seventy-by-fifty-five-mile rectangle of land, thus outnumbering the Hopi on their own reservation. In addition, the order creating the reservation included wording that would allow non-Hopis to live there. So the establishment of the reservation solved nothing and in fact set the stage for future trouble.

Additional Settlement

More Navajo continued to settle in the Hopi Reservation, and the government did nothing to stop them. In fact, some government agents quietly encouraged the Navajo to do so. For one thing, the Navajo needed more space and Anglo ranchers did not want their reservation expanded. For another, most Bureau of Indian Affairs (BIA) officials thought the

Use of the Land

Part of the argument for allowing the Navajo to settle on the Hopi Reservation was that the Hopi were not "using" the land. The Hopi defined land use in different terms. Susan Sekaquaptewa, wife of the tribal chairman, wrote about this difference in an editorial in 1980. It is found in *The Second Long Walk* by Jerry Kammer.

"Repeatedly you hear at these meetings that it is politically necessary to use the HPL [Hopi Partition Lands] to secure it for the Hopis. Otherwise someday the "great white father" in Washington, D.C. will look over it and say, 'I don't see any Hopis or Hopi livestock or activity on the land, so we'll give it back to the Navajos or just keep letting the Navajos stay.' The Hopis always respond that they use the land in a special sense, that it has spiritual value and meaning and that by hunting for eagles and foxes and servicing the shrines they are using the land. It is a different definition of 'land use' than the *bahana* one but it is just as valid and important in context of Hopi culture and religion. Unfortunately, *bahanas* are in charge and are very practical and pragmatic, and if they have an excess of Navajos who need land, or stoves without fuel they might easily bulldoze over this gentle passive type of land use and seize it for their own purpose."

Hopi Reservation contained far more land than necessary for the Hopi. This was equally true among those who worked directly with the Hopi and who had failed in efforts to get them to move from their mesa-top villages.

Hopi agent Leo Crane, while he despised the Hopi's desire to hold fast to their traditions, nevertheless wanted to keep the Navajo away from them. Yet he, like others, viewed the Navajo as progressive and industrious and the Hopi as mired in the past. He proposed that half the reservation, about 1.25 million acres, be set aside strictly for Hopi use for ten years. If, after that time, the Hopi had not used the land, it would be open to the Navajo. The Hopi, said Crane, "should not be permitted to eject an industrious (if disobedient) neighbor and then allow the land to waste and his [the Hopi's] sheep to decline in filthy mesa corrals while he indulges in snake dances, basket dances, clown dances, and the 10,000 other displays he uses as an excuse why he should not be on the range."[21]

The Indian agents, however, viewed "use" in a very different sense from the Hopi. The federal employees looked at land as a tool or resource to serve the people. The Hopi, on the other hand, saw themselves as having a sacred kinship with the land and believed that they had been assigned by the gods to be guardians of the Fourth World. As Abbot Sekaquaptewa, former chairman of the Hopi Tribal Council, said, "We were given the land around the mesas by the giver of the breath of life. And it was given to us for good reasons. We need those lands for our culture, our religious life, our sense of belonging. Hopi people feel they have a purpose for being here on this earth. They have been called on to maintain a stewardship over Mother Earth."[22]

Why, he asks, must Hopi "use" of the land be judged by the white man's criteria?

The Hopi View

This basic lack of understanding of the Hopi's relationship with the land has remained the underlying cause of the dispute. The Hopi maintain that the land was given to them in trust by the gods. It is their *tusqua*, site of their sacred places. It is bad enough, they say, that some sacred areas such as the Grand Canyon and San Francisco Mountains have been taken from them, but the Navajo want to take most of what remains.

The Navajo practice of copying and selling traditional Hopi crafts has angered the Hopi. Pictured are kachina dolls on display at a Navajo trading post.

In addition, the Hopi complain that the Navajo want to take more than land away from them. They claim the Navajo are stealing their culture. Sekaquaptewa complained, for instance, that the Navajo have made the San Francisco Mountains a sacred spot, although they were nowhere near them until comparatively recent times.

The Navajo have also copied traditional Hopi crafts, carving kachinas and selling them to tourists at prices lower than Hopi works. "Some of them even make prayer feathers now," Sekaquaptewa said. "I can't make prayer feathers because I'm not a priesthood person . . . so here I am a Hopi and I can't make prayer feathers but some Navajo in Ganado [a Navajo town] can make prayer feathers."[23]

Economic Factors

The Hopi desire to expel the Navajo from the *tusqua* has not been entirely spiritual in nature. The so-called Progressives have long been interested in the wealth that its mineral deposits might bring. Also, some of the more well-to-do Hopi have wanted to extend the range for their cattle to areas far distant from the mesas.

The government did take some action to try to keep the Navajo from getting too close to the mesas. In 1891 the Navajo were forbidden to live or graze their flocks within sixteen miles of the central village

The Navajo Threat

Hopi tribal chairman Abbot Sekaquaptewa described the threat of the Navajo to his people in an 1895 interview. This excerpt is found in *The Wind Won't Know Me* by Emily Benedek.

"The natural environment doesn't belong to the Hopis. They belong to it—they are a part of it, therefore they respect the things of nature—or they did. But now, there are some doubts that are being created among the younger people because of two things—they're not learning these things from the elders, or the elders aren't teaching them

these things anymore. And at the same time they're going to school in a high-tech world that teaches them technology but not the knowledge of life. So, these cultural things, spiritual things, ceremonial things are beginning to erode. . . . Unless things are done to protect the Hopi as Hopi the Navajo Tribe will swallow up the Hopi Tribe. And it's only a matter of time. Hopi society will become a part of Navajo society. There will be no more Hopi society. It's like throwing ten gallons of white paint into 180 gallons of blue paint. It's going to look real blue by the time you get through fixing it up."

John Collier (right), commissioner of Indian Affairs, is accompanied by Hopi chiefs at a Washington, D.C., ceremony.

of Mishongnovi, and the boundary was marked. Although the boundary encompassed only about a fifth of the reservation—519,000 acres—the Navajo simply ignored it.

Finally, as the growing numbers of sheep and cattle threatened to ruin the entire reservation, John Collier, commissioner of the BIA from 1933 to 1945, took action. He saw that overgrazing would soon render the land unfit for any kind of agriculture and force both the Hopi and Navajo to abandon the reservation and try to learn the ways of the white man's

world. He ordered that all flocks and herds be reduced.

The stock reduction program hit both tribes hard. It began with an across-the-board 10 percent reduction and grew from there. In 1942, for example, the government called for the number of Hopi-owned sheep to be reduced by 24 percent by the following year. The numbers for the Navajo were even higher. The Indians were paid for their livestock, but only for the value of the meat, not—for example— for the value of the wool a sheep would produce year after year.

As part of the stock reduction program, the government divided the Navajo and Hopi reservations into eighteen grazing districts and calculated the number of livestock that each district would support. In 1943 District 6, an area surrounding the mesas roughly equivalent to the 1891 boundary, was designated for the Hopi's exclusive use. Everything else was opened to the Navajo. The Hopi Reservation had, in effect, been reduced by almost 80 percent.

Healing v. Jones

The Hopi refused to recognize the legality of their confinement to District 6. Years of protests got them nowhere, so in 1956 the Hopi Tribal Council filed suit against the government to regain the entire 1882 reservation. The Navajo promptly filed a suit of their own, claiming about 80 percent of the same land. Since the government, by law, has to give its consent before being sued, the case went to Congress. In 1956 Congress passed legislation that allowed the two tribes to file a joint suit to determine their rights.

The case, called *Healing v. Jones* after the two tribal chairmen at the time, was heard by a three-judge panel in Prescott, Arizona, in 1960. The Hopi asserted that the land had been granted to them in 1882, that this was their ancestral home, and that the Navajo had no right to be there. The Navajo countered that their ancestors were living on the land before 1882 and that they were the "other Indians" mentioned in the presidential order. Furthermore,

A Hopi elder tribesman rests in the fields where he is working in 1960, the year that the controversial land dispute case Healing v. Jones *was heard in court.*

they said, a Hopi victory would mean the forced relocation of thousands of Navajo.

The judges ruled in 1962 that the government had never officially settled the Navajo on the Hopi Reservation. Furthermore, Hopi failure to expand into more of the reservation was attributed partially to a fear of the much more powerful Navajo. The Hopi were given exclusive rights to District 6, and the rest of the reservation was to be a Joint Use Area (JUA) over which the tribes were to have "joint, undivided and equal rights and interest."[24]

This decision gave neither tribe what it wanted and was guaranteed to cause more trouble in the future. The Hopi continued to argue that the concept of joint use was unworkable, that the Navajo would continue to dominate most of the land. The only way to preserve the *Healing v. Jones* decision, they said, was partition. The Navajo, on the other hand, vowed they would not be relocated.

The Land Settlement Act

After a long battle in Congress during which both the Hopi and Navajo waged public relations and lobbying campaigns, the Hopi won. On December 22, 1974, Public Law 93-531, the Navajo-Hopi Land Settlement Act, called for an equal division of the JUA and the formation of a commission to move people of one tribe off the lands of the other.

The Navajo-Hopi Land Settlement Act, while a defeat for the Navajo, still was not a complete victory for the Hopi. They had won back half their reservation, but many still thought they should have received all the reservation. The Traditionalists, moreover, recognized no reservation boundaries, but thought the Hopi deserved all the ancient *tusqua*.

Congress left the actual division of the reservation to a federal district court, which assigned the job to mediator William Simkin. Simkin presided over the negotiations between the two tribes, which were predictably difficult. At one point, for instance, the Navajo said the Hopi should accept their version of a partition map because "had it not been for the grace and forbearance of the Navajos, the Hopi Tribe would not even exist today."[25]

In 1975 Simkin suggested a dividing line that he called "a surveyor's nightmare."[26] It satisfied neither tribe. In order to relocate as few Navajo as possible, Simkin had created a Navajo island around the mostly Navajo community of Jeddito and a finger of land jutting into Hopi territory to take in the Navajo settlement at Hardrock.

The Simkin line was formally adopted on February 10, 1977, and trouble started immediately. Hopi chairman Sekaquaptewa ordered Hopi policemen to seize Navajo cattle on what had been ruled Hopi land. It seemed for a time that violence might erupt, but the government eased the crisis by agreeing that all Navajo livestock would be off Hopi land within a year.

Difficulty of Relocation

The question of moving Navajo people was much more difficult. The Hopi on the

Graffiti on a Hopi reservation rock outcrop reflects the persisting hostility the tribe harbors toward their Navajo neighbors.

Navajo Partition Lands (NPL) moved quickly, but there were only a few hundred. Conversely, several thousand Navajo were on land that had been awarded to the Hopi.

The government created a three-member Relocation Commission to oversee the process. A deadline of July 6, 1986, was established for all relocation to be completed. The commission, however, was plagued by internal bickering and by criticism from both tribes—the Hopi saying relocation was going too slowly and the Navajo resisting all attempts to move them. At the end of eighteen months, the commission had spent $180,000 and had actually relocated only a few dozen Navajo.

Under pressure from Congress, the commission sped up its efforts. Still, by 1985 the task was only one-third completed. Congress extended the deadline "until such time as housing is acquired for those families still on the Hopi Partitioned Lands."[27] The problem was that there was little room and few jobs on the NPL or on the Navajo reservation for those to be relocated.

The Relocation Amendment Act

Some progress had been made in 1980 with the passage by Congress of the Navajo and Hopi Indian Relocation

Amendment Act. The act allowed the transfer of 250,000 acres of public land to the Navajo and allowed them to buy 150,000 more acres in New Mexico. The Hopi also yielded somewhat by supporting the part of the act that allowed up to 120 Navajo who had been forty-nine years old or older in 1974 to have "life estates" of ninety acres. This meant they could continue living on the HPL until they died.

The Hopi agreement to the life estates was not entirely for humanitarian reasons. The Navajo, with the help of public relations companies, had succeeded in arousing considerable nationwide sympathy for those facing relocation. The Hopi, who had admitted they wanted the HPL partially for cattle grazing, did not want to project an image of putting cattle ahead of the old people's right to stay in their homes.

Far more people than the 120 maximum permitted by the act sought to take advantage of the life estates. In 1992 the Hopi and Navajo, after considerable negotiation, reached the Accommodation Agreement. Navajo families still on the HPL could remain on a seventy-five-year lease, after which they must move to the NPL. The agreement was ratified by Congress in 1996.

The Trauma of Relocation

This analysis of the likely effect of relocation on the Navajo was made by Dr. David Aberle, an anthropologist at the University of British Columbia. It is found in *The Navajo-Hopi Land Dispute* by David M. Brugge.

"There is a sense in which one need not know anything about past relocation efforts, nor anything about Navajo culture, kinship or economy, to be able to anticipate the outcome of relocation. If 8,000 inter-related human beings, living where their ancestors have lived for centuries, are thrust from their homeland under these conditions, it can be expected that they will resist relocation. Such a reaction has nothing specific to do with Navajo culture or personality; it is an expectable human response. Deprived of livestock, crowded onto the reservation, moved into new territory that lacks what is needed to render it habitable, the relocates will be impoverished, dislocated, disorganized and dependent. Those whom they crowd will be resentful and will also be economically impaired. The relocates will lose faith in their tribal government and be alienated from the Federal Government. Years of economic dependency, administrative problems, and waste of human potential can be foreseen."

A Navajo supporter holds up barbed wire from a partition fence on the Hopi Reservation torn down by protesters demonstrating in 1986 against Navajo relocation.

Most of the Navajo bowed to what they considered to be inevitable, either moving to the NPL or signing a seventy-five-year lease. However, a handful—mostly in the Big Mountain area in the northeast HPL—continued to resist. They filed suit, claiming that relocation amounted to religious discrimination. The Ninth Circuit Court of Appeals ruled against the Navajo in June 1999, and the U.S. Supreme Court dismissed the case in April 2001.

In 2002 only about three hundred Navajo remained on the HPL out of the thousands who once lived there. Most—those who have life estates or have signed leases—are tolerated by the Hopi even if they are not entirely welcome. The Hopi are much less tolerant of the Navajo who remain on their lands illegally. Until what remains of the 1882 Hopi Reservation is entirely free of the Navajo, tension between the tribes is very likely to continue.

Chapter 8

Old Ways, New Times

The Hopi have always been good borrowers. As the clans gathered at the mesas, the talents of each new group were used to make the society stronger. The Hopi borrowed much from the Spaniards and missionaries that was helpful without surrendering their religion in the process. They have likewise learned profitable new ways from the Americans, but the challenge for the Hopi in the twenty-first century is to keep their traditions from being overwhelmed by outside cultural forces.

The Hopi's best friend in the borrowing process has been their isolation, but that isolation is rapidly disappearing. News and entertainment from the Anglo world is available on cable and satellite television. Those tending crops or flocks may well carry a cellular telephone along with their other tools. Distance is no longer an effective shield against the outside world.

Appearance Unchanged

Modern innovations, however, have done little to change the appearance of the *tusqua.* Walpi, Sichimovi, and Hano maintain their perches atop First Mesa, with Polacca below. Shungopovi, Mishongnovi, and Shipolovi are on Second Mesa. Orabi, largely in ruins, lies on the lip of Third Mesa with Kykotsmovi ("New Orabi") on the plain below. Hotevilla and Bakavi, both offshoots of Orabi after the bitter split in 1906, are west of Orabi on Third Mesa. Further west are the last villages, Upper Moencopi and Lower Moencopi, settled by Hopi with help from the Mormons.

To the east is Keams Canyon, the only remaining settlement at Antelope Mesa. Although the headquarters of the Bureau of Indian Affairs Agency and Tribal Council, it is not considered a Hopi village. It has no *kikmongwi,* no ceremonies and, perhaps as a result, is the most modern-looking spot on the reservation. A large trading post sits on the highway alongside a combination gas station and convenience store. The modern junior-senior high school located nearby would not be out of place in any American city.

Two young Hopi boys stand atop a Third Mesa rock formation on the Hopi Reservation.

These trappings of the Anglo world are found nowhere else on the Hopi Reservation. There are tiny stores here and there, most operated out of private homes. But while the lack of modern shopping facilities may give the villages a traditional appearance, it is also a sign of one of the Hopi's most pressing problems—lack of employment.

Unemployment

Only about 40 percent of the Hopi have full-time jobs, and 27 percent are unemployed as compared to the overall unemployment rate in Arizona of 4.4 percent. Few stores means few retail jobs. Periodic attempts to establish factories on the reservation have not been successful. And,

while some Hopi commute to Holbrook, Winslow, or Flagstaff, many have found it hard to keep jobs in the Anglo world because of religious obligations. The frequency and length of Hopi ceremonies do not mesh well with the demands of a Monday through Friday workweek.

Agriculture, while it does not dominate the Hopi economy as before, remains important. Corn, as always, is the primary crop not only for food but also for ceremonies. Yellow corn represents knowledge. Blue denotes patience. Red signifies respect and white, purity. Hopi elder Edmund Nequatewa explains, "With the Hopi, corn comes first in all ceremonies as he believes it is in his heart, his life and his food. . . . Ears of corn are of different colors and not only must the colors be true, but the ears must be perfect."[28]

For the most part, however, the Hopi grow corn, beans, squash, peaches, apricots, and other fruits and vegetables for their own family's use. They sell or trade some surplus, but there are few cash crops. Livestock, however, has become much more important to the economy. With the recovery of large parts of the reservation from the Navajo, sheep and cattle ranching has expanded. This expansion caused some critics to say that the Hopi desire to reclaim their land was just as much economic as religious. Yet, even with the growth in ranching, agriculture accounts for only about 20 percent of the Hopi economy.

Casino Rejected

In 1995 the Hopi voted to reject a proposal to build a casino on Hopi-owned land in Winslow. Progressives argued that it would be an economic boost. Traditionalists said that it was counter to the Hopi Way. Former tribal chairman Ivan Sidney said, "Our people are taught to work the honest way. We believe that we are the last to hold a strong and complete tradition, and that if we fall, it will be the end of Native American traditions in this country."[29]

The campaign was divisive and emphasized the continuing philosophical differences among the Hopi. It caused such bad feelings, something most Hopi try to

A farmer uses a hand plow to prepare a field for planting corn, which has retained its importance to the Hopi for food and ceremonial purposes.

avoid, that the election took place on the condition that the results would be binding and permanent, meaning the issue could never come up again. The final vote was close, 714 for the casino and 986 against.

Part of the argument by the Traditionalists against the casino was that, should it prove profitable, the Tribal Council could not be trusted to spend the profits for everyone's benefit. Such a stance pointed out yet another ongoing Hopi concern. Although the Tribal Council is the reservation's biggest employer—about 40 percent of all jobs including police, health and welfare workers, and teachers—many Hopi have never recognized it as legitimate. The tradition of each village being self-governing is strong, and the more conservative villages refuse to send representatives to the council.

And yet most money coming to the tribe from outside sources—mineral leases, grazing rights, government funds, rentals from Hopi-owned property off the reservation—is funneled through the Tribal Council. While much of the money is spent directly on social services, education, and public works, Traditionalists question other expenditures such as off-reservation real estate and the fees paid to attorneys to recover lands that, the Traditionalists claim, will benefit only a few.

Leases Questioned

Many Hopi also question the mineral leases, both the uses made of the profits and the effects on the environment. The first leases were signed in 1961 with com-

panies drilling for oil—unsuccessfully, as it turned out. Coal, however, was a far different matter. The Hopi had been mining deposits near the surface for centuries, and geologists knew that one of the nation's largest coal fields lay below the Hopi and Navajo reservations.

In 1969 the Navajo and Hopi signed a long-term lease with the Peabody Coal Company. A total of forty thousand acres was on Navajo land; twenty-five thousand were on the Joint Use Area. After the division of the JUA, the two tribes agreed to divide income from the lease, estimated in 1988 at more than $10 million per year.

Profitable though it is, coal mining on the Hopi Reservation has raised three concerns. One is the use to which the Tribal Council puts the income. The other two are environmental. Some of the coal has been used to power huge electric power generators. In 1971 astronauts took a photograph from an altitude of 170 miles. The only man-made object visible was a huge plume of smoke from one of these plants. The people of Shongopovi complained that the haze was so bad that they could not properly time the sunrise to set the dates for ceremonies.

The second environmental concern involved an age-old Hopi problem—water. To move the coal Peabody uses a 275-mile-long pipeline carrying "slurry," a mixture half water, half coal, to a power plant in Nevada. Many Hopi and Navajo claim that the enormous amount of water used— 3 million gallons a day according to the Natural Resources Defense Council—is

A Navajo woman speaks out at a rally against the Peabody Coal Company, whose mining on Hopi and Navajo lands has raised environmental concerns.

depleting the underground aquifer that is the main water source for both tribes. The company denies this, citing scientific studies that show the Indians' water comes from a different source.

To resolve the issue the Hopi and Navajo have joined to try to force the government to close the slurry line. They also are requesting the government to build another pipeline that would furnish both tribes freshwater from Lake Powell, just across the border in southern Utah.

Concern over Tourism

Tourists pose another concern. To the Hopi, particularly the Traditionalists, they are a mixed blessing. Certainly they are

nothing new. Ever since the late 1800s the picturesque villages and elaborate colorful ceremonies have been magnets that have drawn artists, scientists, and the merely curious.

At first the Hopi welcomed all outsiders to all but the most secret ceremonies. They permitted photography. They reasoned that since their prayers were for all people, not only the Hopi, all people would benefit from attending the rituals.

Eventually, however, crowds grew too large and showed little respect, treating the ceremonies more as entertainment than something spiritual. Photographs of such ceremonies as the Snake Dance were used to demonstrate how "barbaric" the Hopi were. As a result the Hopi banned photography of ceremonies in the early 1900s and finally prohibited photography anywhere on the reservation by non-Hopi. Today, while some of the social dances are open to the public, outsiders can attend kachina dances only by invitation and only in a few villages while others are completely closed to non-Indians.

The Hopi philosophy and reputation as a peaceful people have been an attraction for some people. In the late 1960s many so-called hippies developed a romantic idea of the Hopi lifestyle and came to the reservation thinking they would find lives of peace and harmony with nature.

More recently, in the 1990s, people promoting "New Age" ideas concluded that their philosophy was much like that of the Hopi. The Hopi have received such visitors and their ideas with an amused toleration. Some believers in reincarnation, for instance, have claimed that they were Hopi in former lives. This type of physical reincarnation, however, is not part of Hopi tradition. Gary Tso, a highly regarded kachina carver who also serves as a guide to reservation visitors, said, "Sometimes I want to tell these people, 'Look, you're not my Anasazi ancestor. You're just a mixed-up *bahana* from Massachusetts.'"[30]

The Tourism Economy

Even though tourists may be bothersome, they account for a very important part of the economy—as much as 60 percent. They spend money at the motel and restaurant, they tour the villages and attend what dances they can. Mostly, however, they buy the artworks and crafts for which the Hopi are famous—baskets, pottery, kachinas, and silver jewelry.

Crowds wait for the start of a Snake Dance in 1899. In the early 1900s the Hopi began banning photography of ceremonies and limiting the number of outside spectators.

Protecting the Earth

Soon after the Hopi and Navajo tribes signed a long-term mineral lease with the Peabody Coal Company, a group of environmentalists and Hopi Traditionalists filed a lawsuit to halt the mining. In a statement accompanying the suit, found in *The Second Long Walk* by Jerry Kammer, the Hopi said,

"We, the Hopi leaders, have watched as the white man has destroyed his land, his water, and his air. The white man has made it harder for us to maintain our traditional ways and religious life. Now for the first time we have decided to intervene in the white man's court to prevent the final devastation. We should not have had to go this far. Our words have not been heeded. We can no longer watch as our sacred lands are wrested from our control and as our spiritual center disintegrates. We cannot allow our spiritual homelands to be taken from us. The hour is already late."

Basketry is the oldest of the crafts, dating from the Hopi ancestors' remote past. The most common baskets, made by women on all three mesas, are the sifters, woven out of yucca leaves and used primarily in the home as a carry-all and for sifting corn meal. In addition, the women on Second Mesa make coiled baskets from grasses and yucca, and Third Mesa artists specialize in wicker baskets made mostly of sumac branches and rabbitbrush twigs.

Plaques, round trays both coiled and wicker, are very popular tourist items, the best selling for up to one thousand dollars. They are valuable to the Hopi for other reasons. Some are used to carry sacred cornmeal in ceremonies, and a bride's family traditionally weaves a plaque for the groom—the *hahawpi*—on which his spirit will descend to the underworld after death.

Pottery is another ancient Hopi craft. It declined as an art form after the Spanish came and was all but lost after metal pots and pans became available in the 1800s. Its recovery, almost by accident, has had great significance to the economy.

The pottery tradition was revived in 1895 when archaeologist Jessie Fewkes was exploring the ruins of Sityatki at First Mesa. One of his Hopi workers took some of the colorful fragments he found to his wife, Nampeyo. One of the few women who still made pottery, she was fascinated by the designs and at Fewkes's urging began to incorporate them into her work. Experimenting, she found that firing, or baking, her pots packed in sheep dung gave them a warm, yellow orange luster.

Basketry is the oldest Hopi craft, and the tribe's unique designs are popular with tourists.

Nampeyo's pottery was unlike anything seen by the Hopi in three hundred years. Tourists began paying high prices for it, and soon other women on First Mesa began copying Nampeyo's technique. She died in 1942, but her tradition has been carried on by generations of First Mesa women including her daughters, granddaughters, and great-granddaughters. In recent years, as the prices of Hopi pottery have risen, men have turned their hands to this once all-female craft. Good quality Hopi pots sell for three hundred to five hundred dollars, and works by the better-known artists can bring ten times as much.

Kachina Carving

Kachina carving is another ancient Hopi craft that has found a very enthusiastic modern audience. It has long been customary to teach young girls about the kachina ceremonies by giving them *tihu*, or dolls, that represent the various spirits. Significantly, the tihu are symbols of the kachinas and thus are not considered sacred objects as are, for example, prayer sticks or kachina masks. Even so, some traditional Hopi oppose their being made strictly for sale to outsiders.

Kachina carvings are usually done from the roots of cottonwood trees. Before they

Nampeyo's Legacy

The redevelopment of classic Hopi pottery by Nampeyo had a lasting effect on the Hopi economy and also was a significant contribution to the world of art. Mary-Russell Colton and Harold Colton of the Museum of Northern Arizona wrote this assessment, found in *Pages from Hopi History* by Harry C. James.

"Nampeyo in her early days, may have made replicas of Sityatki pottery, though this is extremely doubtful as the Indian artists rarely make an exact copy. However, it is certain that the vessels that came on the market were not mere copies but had a living quality of their own. She caught the spirit of the old Sityatki potters and used her own rare good taste in making compositional arrangement.

Her work was distinguished from that of Hopi potters by a sense of freedom and a fluid flowing quality of design, together with an appreciation of space as a background for her bold rhythmic forms.

Nampeyo's interest did not confine itself to design and its application, but also included the basic characteristic of Sityatki and other fine forms not heretofore in use.

Before Nampeyo's time, the Hopi potters' art was slowly fading. . . . The financial success of Nampeyo stimulated a host of other women, including her own daughters, to use prehistoric motifs. This type of Hopi pottery soon was manufactured in great volume and was traded to the outside world."

Nampeyo displays examples of her skilled artistry.

Intricate Hopi kachina carvings, like these Snake and Antelope priest figures, are popular collectors' items and often fetch high prices.

keeping with Hopi tradition, the highly detailed carvings command the highest prices, more than ten thousand dollars in galleries in Phoenix and Santa Fe.

Silversmithing is not a traditional Hopi art form, but their silverwork began to find a market after 1938 when Mary-Russell Colton of the Museum of Northern Arizona urged the Hopi to find a style that would differentiate their work from that of the Navajo. The result was "overlay," a technique whereby designs are painstakingly cut from thin silver plates with a wire saw. The artist then "sweats," or solders, the designs onto a second sheet of silver and textures the surrounding area to make the designs stand out.

Because it rarely contains gemstones, Hopi jewelry is relatively inexpensive. A top-quality belt buckle will be priced at about $350 and most pieces are much less, although those using gold or gems can be much more expensive.

Income and Poverty

Although many Hopi make their living as artists, only the best make a good living, at least by Anglo standards. The official Hopi Internet site gives the average per capita income as $17,521, higher than the average for the state of Arizona. Yet the same summary says that 56.5 percent of

drew the attention of tourists and collectors, carvings were flat and smooth with no separation of the limbs from the body. Gradually, in response to buyer preference, carvers began making their figures more lifelike down to the tiniest detail.

Lately there has been somewhat of a return to more traditional forms, but although these plainer versions are more in

the Hopi are below the poverty line as defined by the U.S. Department of Health and Human Services.

Part of this apparent contradiction is because official statistics on Native Americans—and the Hopi are no exception—seldom present an accurate picture. Most Traditionalists and a large percentage of older people want nothing to do with the U.S. government and refuse to complete census forms. Many also distrust the Tribal Council, but the surveys taken by Hopi officials are probably much more accurate than the U.S. census.

Official Hopi figures as of October 2001 show a total membership of 11,156, of which about 9,000 live on the reservation. U.S. census figures, on the other hand, show only about 6,800 Hopi on the reservation. Unlike other Native American tribes, the percentage living on the reservation has increased over the last decade.

The fact that Hopi are not leaving but staying on, and even returning to, the *tusqua* is an indication that they are holding their own against outside forces. The Hopi seem to be succeeding in maintaining the essence of their traditions in spite of being surrounded and vastly outnumbered. They have maintained their pride. Only 16 percent of those unemployed have chosen to receive government aid.

Maintaining the Way

The Hopi have endured. They were not turned from the Hopi Way by Spanish

Choosing Carefully

The Hopi have been adept at taking from other cultures aspects that will benefit them without destroying their traditions. Richard O. Clemmer discussed recent examples of this practice in his book *Roads in the Sky.*

"Through structures created by Washington that were preadapted for metropolis-satellite political economic relationships, Hopis' allocations of time, energy, and resources were turned from farming to stock raising and then to wage labor, industrial activities, and the creation of political bureaucracies modeled on U.S. examples. Acknowledging this point does not eliminate the possibilities of Hopis pursuing their own goals. Modernization includes the process of pursuing goals, directly or indirectly, through rational methods. Hopis have learned a new twist to this process because they have pursued goals obliquely [indirectly] as well as directly, with a sophistication and a degree of success rarely matched by any other minority within a pluralistic society."

Hopi students at Hotevilla Day School. Hopi youth must find ways to preserve their culture despite increasing influence from outside forces.

soldiers or priests, by American missionaries, teachers, and government officials. They have remained faithful guardians of the land given to them in trust by the gods after their emergence from the Third World. They have endured much and, if they must endure more, so be it.

In 1916 government agent Leo Crane built a school in Hotevilla. Yokeoma, who had led the Hostiles from Orabi ten years earlier, had not ceased his opposition to the government. He protested sending children to the new school so vigorously that Crane had him jailed. From his cell, the old chief told the agent, "I shall go home sometime. Washington may send another Agent to replace you, or you may return to your own people, as all men do. Or you may be dismissed by the government. Those things have happened before. White men come into the desert; but the Hopi, who come from the Underworld, remain."[31]

Notes

Chapter 2: The Hopi Way

1. Quoted in Don Talayesva, *Sun Chief: The Autobiography of a Hopi Indian,* ed. Leo Simmons. New Haven, CT: Yale University Press, 1942, p. 17.

Chapter 3: Life on the Mesas

2. Quoted in Robert C. Euler and Henry F. Dobyns, *The Hopi People.* Phoenix, AZ: Indian Tribal Series, 1971, p. 86.

Chapter 4: The Spaniards

3. Quoted in Harry C. James, *Pages from Hopi History.* Tucson: University of Arizona Press, 1974, p. 36.
4. Quoted in James, *Pages from Hopi History,* p. 38.
5. Quoted in James, *Pages from Hopi History,* p. 41.
6. Quoted in James, *Pages from Hopi History,* p. 42.
7. Quoted in James, *Pages from Hopi History,* p. 45.
8. Quoted in James, *Pages from Hopi History,* p. 47.

Chapter 5: The Americans

9. Quoted in James, *Pages from Hopi History,* p. 101.
10. Quoted in Euler, *The Hopi People,* p. 61.

11. Quoted in Frank Waters, *Book of the Hopi.* New York: Ballantine Books, 1963, p. 376.
12. Quoted in Waters, *Book of the Hopi,* p. 376.
13. Quoted in James, *Pages from Hopi History,* p. 165.

Chapter 6: The Missionaries

14. Quoted in James, *Pages from Hopi History,* p. 86.
15. Quoted in James, *Pages from Hopi History,* p. 87.
16. Quoted in Thomas E. Mails and Dan Evehema, *Hotevilla: Hopi Shrine of the Covenant, Microcosm of the World.* New York: Marlowe, 1995, p. 224.
17. Quoted in Lois Barrett, *The Vision and the Reality.* Newton, KS: Faith and Life Press, 1983, p. 41.
18. Quoted in James, *Pages from Hopi History,* p. 150.
19. Quoted in Barrett, *The Vision and the Reality,* p. 49.

Chapter 7: The Navajo

20. Quoted in Jerry Kammer, *The Second Long Walk.* Albuquerque: University of New Mexico Press, 1980, p. 70.
21. Quoted in Kammer, *The Second Long Walk,* p. 31.

22. Quoted in Emily Benedek, *The Wind Won't Know Me*. New York: Alfred A. Knopf, 1992, p. 39.

23. Quoted in Benedek, *The Wind Won't Know Me*, p. 41.

24. Quoted in David M. Brugge, *The Navajo-Hopi Land Dispute*. Albuquerque: University of New Mexico Press, 1994, p. 97.

25. Quoted in Kammer, *The Second Long Walk*, p. 154.

26. Quoted in Benedek, *The Wind Won't Know Me*, p. 153.

27. Quoted in Yee S'ee: The Official Web Site of the Hopi Tribe, "History of the Navajo-Hopi Land Dispute." www. hopi.nsn.us.

Chapter 8: Old Ways, New Times

28. Edmund Nequatewa, quoted as part of display on the Hopi, Heard Museum, Phoenix, AZ, December 2001.

29. Quoted in Miriam Davidson, "Hopis Balk at Blackjack, Dance to Different Drum," *Christian Science Monitor,* 1995, Hopi Information Network. www. recycles.org.

30. Interview with the author, Second Mesa, AZ, September 2, 2001.

31. Quoted in Benedek, *The Wind Won't Know Me*, p. 124.

For Further Reading

Books

Nancy Bonvillain, *The Hopi.* New York: Chelsea House, 1994. Excellent overview of Hopi history and culture for younger readers.

Harold Courlander, *People of the Short Blue Corn.* Illus. Enrico Arno. New York: Harcourt Brace Jovanovich, 1970. Series of short folk tales that spring from Hopi traditions.

Jennifer Owings Dewey, *Rattlesnake Dances.* Honesdale, PA: Boyds Mill Press, 1997. Bitten by a rattler at age nine, the author weaves personal reminiscences and facts about rattlesnakes. Included is an eyewitness account of a Hopi Snake Dance.

Franklin Folsom, *Indian Uprising on the Rio Grande: The Pueblo Revolt of 1680.* Illus. J.D. Roybal. Albuquerque: University of New Mexico Press, 1996. Award-winning account of rebellion is told from the Native American point of view, comparing their motives to that of American colonists in 1776.

Arthur Day Grove, *Coronado's Quest.* Berkeley and Los Angeles: University of California Press, 1982. Reprint of the 1940 book on Coronado's explorations. Long, yet highly readable book for the serious student.

Gene Meany Hodge, *Kachina Tales from the Indian Pueblos.* Santa Fe, NM: Sunstone Press, 1993. Series of stories originally published in the 1930s about the relationship of these spirits with the gods, the Hopi, and one another.

Barbara Kramer, *Nampeyo and Her Pottery.* Illus. James Kramer. Albuquerque: University of New Mexico Press, 1996. Color photographs and maps accompany this biography and evaluation of the great Hopi potter.

Ekkehart Malotki and Michael Lomatuway'ma, *Hopi Coyote Tales: Istutuwutsi.* Illus. Anne-Marie Malotki. Lincoln: University of Nebraska Press, 1984. Delightful stories featuring Coyote, the traditional trickster of Native American folklore. Printed in both English and Hopi.

Marc Simmons, *The Last Conquistador: Juan de Oñate and the Settling of the Far Southwest.* Norman: University of Oklahoma Press, 1991. Impartial description of Spanish explorer-adventurer of whom many Native American tribes have retained bitter memories.

Helga Teiwes, *Hopi Basket Weaving.* Tucson: University of Arizona Press, 1996. Originally written and illustrated for a series of exhibitions in California, book traces development of basketmaking. Contains numerous photographs, some in color.

Barbara Weisberg, *Coronado's Golden Quest.* Illus. Mike Eagle. Austin, TX: Raintree Steck-Vaughn, 1993. Story of Coronado's explorations that highlight the hardships encountered by the Spanish and their determination to find wealth in the New World.

Works Consulted

Books

Lois Barrett, *The Vision and the Reality*. Newton, KS: Faith and Life Press, 1983. Commissioned by the Mennonite church, tells the story of the church's outreach missions throughout North America.

Emily Benedek, *The Wind Won't Know Me*. New York: Alfred A. Knopf, 1992. Penetrating look at the people affected by the forced relocation of the Navajo from the Hopi Reservation.

David M. Brugge, *The Navajo-Hopi Land Dispute*. Albuquerque: University of New Mexico Press, 1994. History of the dispute is written—as the author freely admits—from the Navajo point of view but contains excellent and detailed account of the 1960 Prescott hearings.

Richard O. Clemmer, *Roads in the Sky: The Hopi Indians in a Century of Change*. Boulder, CO: Westview Press, 1995. Very scholarly and detailed examination of the forces bringing change to the Hopi in the twentieth century.

Robert C. Euler and Henry F. Dobyns, *The Hopi People*. Phoenix, AZ: Indian Tribal Series, 1971. One of a series of highly informative books on Native American tribes.

Harry C. James, *Pages from Hopi History*. Tucson: University of Arizona Press, 1974. One of the best sources available on Hopi history after the arrival of the Spaniards. Especially good section on 1880–1930 interactions with Anglo-Americans.

Jerry Kammer, *The Second Long Walk*. Albuquerque: University of New Mexico Press, 1980. Some of the material is dated, but a good, even-handed account of the Hopi-Navajo land dispute.

Frank Kosik, *Native Roads*. Flagstaff, AZ: Creative Solutions, 1996. For tourists, a highly detailed description of the people and places on the Navajo and Hopi reservations.

Charles F. Lummis, *Bullying the Moqui*. Ed. Robert Easton and Mackenzie Brown. Flagstaff, AZ: Prescott College Press, 1968.

Compilation of a series of 1903 articles from Lummis's magazine *Out West* in which he criticizes government treatment of the Hopi.

Thomas E. Mails and Dan Evehema, *Hotevilla: Hopi Shrine of the Covenant, Microcosm of the World.* New York: Marlowe, 1995. Concentrates on Hopi mysticism and prophecy, especially as proclaimed by the Traditionalists at the village of Hotevilla.

Walter Collins O'Kane, *The Hopis: Portrait of a Desert People.* Norman: University of Oklahoma Press, 1953. Interesting series of accounts of interactions with the author and various Hopi in different walks of life.

Ruth DeEtte Simpson, *The Hopi Indians.* Southwest Museum Series, no. 25. Highland Park, CA: Southwest Museum, 1953. Dated, but still packed with information about Hopi history, society, religion, and arts.

Don Talayesva, *Sun Chief: The Autobiography of a Hopi Indian.* Ed. Leo Simmons. New Haven, CT: Yale University Press, 1942. Fascinating first-person story of a Hopi born in 1892 and the changes he saw come to his people.

Frank Waters, *Book of the Hopi.* New York: Ballantine Books, 1963. Concentrates on the religious ceremonialism and philosophy of the Hopi. Excellent account of annual cycle of ceremonies.

Frank Waters, *Masked Gods.* New York: Ballantine Books, 1950. Extensive study of rites and ceremonies among the Navajo and Pueblo tribes of the southwestern United States.

Internet Sources

Miriam Davidson, "Hopis Balk at Blackjack, Dance to Different Drum," *Christian Science Monitor*, 1995, Hopi Information Network. www.recycles.org.

National Resources Defense Council, "Drinking Water Jeopardized in Arizona's Black Mesa Region," October 23, 2000. www.nrdc.org.

Yee S'ee: The Official Web Site of the Hopi Tribe, "History of the Navajo-Hopi Land Dispute." www.hopi.nsn/us.

Index

Picture Credits

Cover: © Kevin Fleming/CORBIS
AP Photo/Robert Spencer, 91
©Bettmann/CORBIS, 64, 74, 86
©Jim Cartier/Photo Researchers, Inc., 98
©Christie's Images/CORBIS, 96
©CORBIS, 27, 95
Courtesy, Colorado Historical Society, William Henry Jackson
    Collection, 24, 32, 37, 38, 52, 56
Cumberland County Historical Society, 62 (both)
The Denver Public Library, 12, 18, 19, 22, 25, 28, 29, 34, 35, 45,
    48, 50, 60, 67, 68, 92
©Kevin Fleming/CORBIS, 79
Hulton/Archive by Getty Images, 40, 54, 57, 66, 82, 94
The National Archives, 77
©Bob Rowan; Progressive Image/CORBIS, 10, 46, 71, 84, 88, 89
Stock Montage, Inc., 43
©Underwood & Underwood/CORBIS, 81
Werner Forman Archive/Art Resource, NY, 17

About the Author

William W. Lace is a native of Fort Worth, Texas. He holds a bachelor's degree from Texas Christian University, a master's from East Texas State University, and a doctorate from the University of North Texas. After working for newspapers in Baytown, Texas, and Fort Worth, he joined the University of Texas at Arlington as sports information director and later became the director of the news service. He is now executive assistant to the chancellor for the Tarrant County College District in Fort Worth. He and his wife, Laura, live in Arlington and have two children. Lace has written numerous other works for Lucent Books, one of which—*The Death Camps* in the Holocaust Library series—was selected by the New York Public Library for its 1999 Recommended Teenage Reading List.

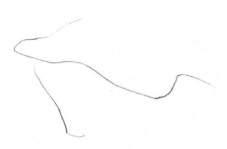